ADVENTURES AND EXPERIENCES WITH GOD

BY

KYLE LEATHERWOOD

Grace Covenant Publishing
Terrell, Texas USA
copyright 2018 all rights reserved

ISBN: 978-1-7320904-0-8

DEDICATION

I dedicate this book to all those who helped me start the first Christian radio station in Freetown, Sierra Leone, West Africa, and the radio station in South Texas.

It would have been impossible to accomplish some of these things if it had not been for the help of specific people in the U.S.A. and in Africa.

I especially want to thank Mrs. Angela Gooding, Ransford Wright, and Mrs. Hannah Dixon, because if it were not for these people, it is quite possible the radio station in Sierra Leone would have stopped operating. I also want to give a special thanks to Dr. Robert Kellum, who taught me a lot in a short period and made a great personal sacrifice for Christ's sake and the gospel.

I want to thank Teddy Hunt, Bruce Tyler and Terry Elder, M. D., who supported the station and me spiritually, physically, and financially. I also thank my wife Veronica and Lee Killgore for their help and sacrifices. Without their help, this book and the radio stations probably would never have happened.

I also want to thank John Osteen, Father Dennis Bennett, Freida Lindsey, Bob Tilton, Lester Sumrall, Kenneth Hagen, Tom Leding, Kenneth Copeland, Rodney Howard Brown, Larry Lea, Joseph Prince and Pat Robertson for their ministerial influence in my life. You will have a part of the fruit through this ministry.

Contents

INTRODUCTION

I would like to include a whole lot of names in this book, but if I did, some people might get killed. The events you are about to read are real life stories and experiences. Some names have been changed to protect the guilty and the innocent. Some events may seem stranger than fiction, but all the stories have been lived by me. In the places where the names of the guilty or innocent could bring consequences such as jail, or possibly, death, the names have been changed. Some stories have been changed enough that I pray no one will receive reprisals from witchcraft societies, Islamic groups, or one of the governments that were in power. I want this book to be a blessing to all and a curse to none.

As you read this book, I hope you are encouraged to obey God, and to do the little things, as well as the big things. Some of the bigger miracles happened, I believe, because I was faithful to the little stuff.

CHAPTER I

SEEKING GOD, BUT NO GOD EXPERIENCE

I was about nine years old lying down, about to go asleep, on the top bunk of the bunk bed that I shared with my older brother, Kirk. My mom came in to say, "Good night". When she came in, out of the blue, Kirk asked my Mom, how do you receive the Lord and be born again. My Mom explained it to him.

I then joined in, not wanting to be left out of the conversation, and she then led us in a prayer to receive Christ. I felt nothing. I was fearful and too insecure, even with my mother, to say I felt nothing and that nothing happened. I should have spoken up but my fears stopped me.

Later, our Pastor, Brother Fineout taught me about receiving the Lord and being water baptized. I thought maybe if I am baptized in water then I will get to have that experience with God that I so much desired. Well, I was baptized and still felt nothing. I was told that I was to believe, even if I felt nothing. I did everything I was told to do, but an experience with God eluded me.

I never experienced anything supernatural or God. I was afraid to tell anyone, for I thought something must be wrong with me since I did not experience anything. I wanted an experience with God, but what I had was a mental acceptance of a spiritual truth. I wanted a real experience.

My best friend was the Pastor's son named, Mark. Mark asked me how I felt after I had been baptized and I said it was great. I lied, I was afraid he would think something was wrong with me.

Honestly, I just felt wet, but it was cool being in the heated baptistery. It was like a big swimming pool. It was fun to play at the church.

I never told anyone I felt like a liar. I knew something must be wrong with me, because I did not really feel anything, or ever had an experience with God. I was told to just accept it by faith. Well, I accepted it by faith; I accepted I was now a Christian even though I never had an experience with God.

As the years passed by, I was at church every Service, Sunday morning, Sunday Night, Wednesday night, Vacation Bible School, and Royal Ambassadors. I even went on visitations sometimes on Tuesday nights to witness to other kids. I was a very good kid trying to please God in every way I knew. But even with all I was doing, there was still no experience with God.

At an assembly in my Elementary school, they had some convicts, dressed in orange prison coveralls, giving their testimonies of all the bad stuff they did, and how they turned to Christ. They shared the experiences they had with the Lord. I was jealous of them. I wanted to have an experience with God too. I had prayed the prayer they talked about, but nothing had ever happened.

A thought came to my mind. "If you want to have an experience with God, you must do some very bad stuff, get wild and then turn to God. If you do that you will have a real experience with God". I knew I tried repeatedly to have an experience with God, but nothing supernatural or real, that I was aware of, ever happened to me.

So, my intellectual mind accepted the solution that came into my mind. I decided to become wild, do lots of bad stuff and then I would turn to the Lord and have a real experience with God.

I know this sounds very stupid to an adult, but to a 12-year-old it made sense. I was the most faithful 12-year-old you would find. I always was good, the teacher's pet, read the Bible, went to church, prayed, but nothing supernatural ever happened. Even after years of doing these things, I never had an experience with God. I never felt the presence of God in any way. So, I decided to change all my friends, "Go wild", and then I will come back to the Lord later and I will be able to have a real experience with God.

I was afraid to tell anyone what was going on inside of me. After all, this logic made perfect sense to me. I was a 12-year-old scholar, spelling champion and had read every biography and autobiography in the school library. I was smart and was usually the teachers favorite. Since I was so trustworthy, I would often have special privileges and special rewards. But what I wanted was an experience with God, where God was visibly working in my life.

CHAPTER II

KIDS GONE WILD

I grew up in what I thought was a Christian home. My half-brother at 18 would fight, yell and be screaming at my mother. All this while my father sat back and did nothing. I remember one time my mother had a broomstick; she was hitting my brother with it. He disobeyed her, which resulted in a fight. Everyone went to church, except my Dad.

Not long after this, my half-brother was arrested for breaking and entering a liquor store. He had robbed a store that sold beer and wine, it was owned by a family friend. He did it so he and his friends could get drunk and have a big party out at the lake at a friend's house.

About the same time, I was a spelling champion in the school and went to the regional spelling contest to represent my school. When I won, even kids at school and at church made fun of me. My parents did not bother with attending the contest to give me emotional support there. The principal of the school drove me there.

When I won the local spelling contest, my reward was KFC chicken, yet when my older brother played football, he got steak. I could easily see the bias for sports over intelligence or academics. I could see everyone thought my half-brother Keith was cool and I was an uncool nerd. This frustrated me. I saw no reward for being good or being smart.

Around this same time, a sexual assault happened to me. I will never forget where I was and how it started, but to tell where and how it started would cause two people's identities to be revealed and possibly cause one to be known as a sexual criminal. I was about 12 years of age when it happened.

I will never forget the eyes of this person that became obsessed with having sex with me; it is as though the person was possessed when this sexual assault happened. The eyes were so intense and driven; they terrified me, even though I knew the person that did this. It was as if there was another person behind the eyes. The person that did this did not have the eyes of the person I knew. They changed right in front of my eyes, as they became entirely consumed with sexual desire. It was scary. Now I believe this was my first experience with someone that was demon possessed at the worst or consumed by hormones at the best. Either way, it was not good.

Years earlier, I had a similar experience with the same type of fear. A great friend of my mother's and of the family would come to our house and play card games. They would always bring Southern Maid donuts from Dallas, anytime they came to visit us. We looked forward to the visits. We all loved this couple; they were so nice and sweet.

Well, they got a divorce and shortly after this divorce, something very bizarre happened. Our friend's ex-husband, VW, the man we knew and trusted, kidnapped two young kids and several days later killed them with a hatchet.

I had spent the night with the man and his wife on several occasions. They both were so sweet and so nice. Yet our family friend was on the news for killing two kids about the same age as me. It was scary for a seven-year-old.

How could the person we knew, do something like this? Something must have made this man become different from the one we knew and loved. What happened to him? We later found out he became a drug addict.

Let's get back to the assault. After I took a shower, on the night of the sexual assault, I returned to the living room. As usual, I was in my underwear with no shirt on. Then my mother asked why I had red marks and bruises on certain parts of my body. I then told her what happened. She became so angry, she began to spank me severely for being involved sexually with someone, even though I had tried to stop it and said no. Even though this other guy raped me, she spanked me for being involved in this. She physically spanked me for a sexual assault against me,

I always respected my mother and those in authority, but when this sexual assault happened, they blamed and punished me. My father did nothing, yet he never did anything to correct us or defend us in any way. No one took my side or believed me, not my father or my mother. This was at the heart of my decision to go wild and change all my friends. If a Christian mother punished you when you were sexually assaulted, what kind of mother and what kind of Christianity was this?

I have forgiven the person that sexually assaulted me, but I will never forget the eyes of the person that did this to me, it was as though they were possessed when the sexual assault happened. The eyes were so intense and driven; they scared me, even though I knew the person that did this.

What could have made this person change and become so obsessed with a need for sex, that they would do this to a 12-year-old? What could have made this other family friend kidnap two kids and kill them?

Not long after this event, many of my cousins were spending the night at my grandmother's house. She let us do just about anything at her house. She would go to bed and we would stay up late watching TV and doing other things. There were boys and girls of different ages. To make a long story short there were probably five kids in the back room with the lights off, wrestling around in the dark. I do not know who started it, but boys and girls were starting to feel each other sexually, grabbing body parts in the dark. We were beginning to play sexually.

Most of the kids were not even teens yet, my grandmother allowed all this to go on in her house and she was a Christian that belonged to the Church of Christ. Family members sometimes used Grandma's back room for sex with girls they brought there at night.

I later learned why she chose to ignore this bad behavior going on right under her roof. All her married life she had to ignore a lot of what her husband my grandfather did. My grandfather "Pappy" died when I was about 8 years old. When I became an adult, I learned he made sexual advances toward several of his daughters- in- law, including my mother. So apparently, my grandmother survived her marriage by ignoring things.

My poor grandfather "Pappy" had worked for my rich grandfather JW, and my rich grandfather had to fire Pappy because of his sexual advances toward all the women customers at the business he owned. It drove his business away. He had to shut it down, in large part because Pappy ruined the reputation of the business since all the customers knew him as a womanizer. In addition, JW's son took money from the business as well. My parents and others told me some of these things. Simply put, the family was dysfunctional.

Within six months of the sexual assault against me, I had changed nearly all my friends and started on a road to becoming wild. I was now going to experience so many things. I would see things and be a part of some things that few ever experienced. It first started out with sex, smoking, and cussing.

Then a cousin talked me into going with them and stealing some cigars from a convenience store. It was exciting, the adrenaline, the heart pounding. Our getaway vehicle was bicycles.

That seemed to be fun, but a few days later, my new friends started a fire and burned down a place. I was not with them. Nevertheless, I became scared for them and myself. What if I was with them and had been caught and sent to jail. So even though I had changed friends, I discovered there were some things even in my wild stage I did not want to do, like starting fires and burning a place down.

Drinking, smoking, cussing, skipping school all became part of my life as a teenager in high school. My parents knew nothing about what was going on and wanted to know nothing. My parents let me stay weekends with my half -brother and his real Dad, Leland.

Leland was my mother's first husband, father of Keith. Leland had even spent some time in a mental hospital. Yet my mother thought it was a great idea for Kirk and me, to go spend some time with my half-brother, his half-brother, and his father.

That weekend Leland tried to show us how to have fun from his perspective. He taught the three of us kids, one being his own son, all barely teens, how to steal from a grocery store without being caught. He would even have contests, to see who could walk out of a store with the most stolen merchandise. In one store, he walked out with about $200 worth of meat. That was a lot of meat back in 1970. He taught us how to avoid being caught when attempting to steal.

My parents had no clue, but they should have known, or maybe they just did not want to know. Leland had been arrested, in jail and even in a mental hospital, but my parents thought it was OK.

One time, three police officers searched me thoroughly and I still walked out of the police station with several stolen items. Charges never filed.

Now since an authority figure was teaching us how to do bad things, a part of me said this is fun and exciting. He told us stories of many different thefts, crimes and things he had done. These stories of crimes were very exciting compared to everyone in my family, by the time I was a senior in high school, I had a very different set of values.

Another of my cousins, when I was about 15, gave us the first drugs and got high with us. We visited his house and he wanted us to try some "killer weed". When we smoked the dope he gave us, I saw it does not make you crazy, as some adults had said. It looked so cool, so I smoked a lot of dope in high school.

In February, my senior year in high school, the principal called me into his office. One of my former teachers, that knew the good kid version of me, talked with me about what was going on in my life. I had missed 58% of the days in school my senior year, but was in the top 10% of my class. Two classes, I did not show up to or report for class, until after 9 weeks. After missing the first 9 weeks of class, I walked into class with papers and did not even get into trouble. I can't explain why, other than grace, being smart and nice, but I usually never got into real trouble.

During my senior year in High School, two of my cousins were into drugs and sometimes sold drugs, so I never had to buy any. This was part of the reason I was skipping school so much. When I did go to school I just slept in class.

Because so many kids made fun of smart kids, I preferred to be known as a druggy or anything, other than smart. I did

11

not want kids to know I was so smart and I succeeded, most did not have a clue. In my circle of friends' smart was laughed at, rebellion against authority in any way was applauded. Doing bad was the way to get acceptance from most of them.

During my senior year in high school, usually I would be smoking dope about 8 hours a day. My cousin was selling it, so I had all I wanted. It was exciting to be in the house with the drugs and people coming to buy from us. We had guns hid around the house. But I began to realize some of the people coming to buy drugs from us, had been frying their brain.

One kid I knew for ten years could no longer hold an intelligent conversation because his brain was fried from hard drug usage. I saw many customers that began to lose brain function from drug use. So, I decided to be a social drug user and only do it with friends occasionally. After all, I did not want to fry my brain with drugs and not be able to accomplish anything with my life. The hard drugs were frying brains. Smoking dope made people so passive they had no drive, ambition or desire to change. I felt as if there was a sense of destiny over my life. I knew inside of me to continue smoking dope so much, would cause me to forfeit my destiny.

Police chases became so common with us, that my brothers outran the police three times in one week. My half-brother taught us how to slow down without using brake lights and many secrets on how to outrun the police. One night several of us were together and the police came up behind us with their lights on. My brother asked me if we should outrun them or stop. I told him let's stop, we do not have any drugs or alcohol and have not gotten into any trouble tonight. So, we stopped.

One of our friends told us some shocking news the next morning, we found out the Highway Patrol had set up a sting operation, to catch us if we ran from the police. Their operation had spikes on the highway and the highway patrol had orders to shoot if necessary to stop us. They were prepared to kill us that night if we ran from them, but that night we stopped. There were many examples of God's grace keeping me alive even though I did not have a clue about it at the time. Even in rebellion against God, God showed his grace, even though at the time I did not recognize God was doing anything.

There were times when I was driving, going over 100 mph, and going fast just for the fun of it, when I had a blowout on the front tire and no problem. Other people I knew had the same thing happen and totaled their vehicles.

One time I was racing at night, going about 120 mph and an electrical overload started a fire and my car was on fire going about 120. It was dark, early morning, about 2 am, on a lone stretch of highway, the car engine went dead, the lights went off, and I coasted to a stop. I opened the hood and literally blew out the fire. There was also the time I was racing with four people in the car, going about 140 mph around a sharp corner with bad tires, halfway drunk and no problem at all. It must have been the grace of God. Now I see God protecting me, but I did not have a clue at the time.

The summers were crazy and wild. Most of these things were exciting, to say the least. It was an adrenaline rush. Plus I thought to my family and friends, it made me look cool, but when you hang out with criminals, sooner or later you must do something serious. One day I went out with my friends and was told we were going to hit several houses, to rob them.

There were four of us. Two of these people were 5 to 10 years older than me, two were "family". I did not know they had a test for me when I went with them that day. They were going to make me rob a place alone, so they could blackmail me, if they needed to later.

My family I could probably handle, but I was not sure about this other guy. He was very connected in organized crime circles. His wife's uncle reportedly was a fence that thieves took the stuff they stole too. He would buy stolen merchandise.

I had seen what these people could do. They could do some real damage to someone, and then there were the stories of very bad things, terrible things they had done to people that crossed them or made them mad, including getting them killed.

They took me to a house, then they told me to get out all by myself and that they would return to pick me up. I was to break in and come back with whatever was of value from the house. I knew their minds were set, you do not say NO to these people. Otherwise, there would be consequences. I tried to show no fear, but I was terrified and did not want to break into this house. I had no choice. I was only 16. These were "my friends". So I did what I was told to do.

When I got into the house they wanted me to rob, I saw these people were Christians and were very poor. There was only a black and white TV, which had no real value. I was so relieved I had a reason not to steal anything. They did not have anything of real value to steal. I had passed their test because I had broken into the house, even if I did not steal anything. They could still blackmail me for breaking and entering or, so I believed.

I did not have a problem when we planned a heist on an organized crime family, or a person dealing in guns on the black market or something similar, but to steal from the poor... I could not bring myself to do it, even if there were consequences.

I had a good friend, Aaron Randall that always told me you could make more money honestly than you could dishonestly. He lived in a three-story house and his Dad had a business. It is true; all the criminals that I knew and would know in the future had less money than my friends that had their own businesses. There was a lot of excitement and adventure in the criminal world, but I personally saw no one getting rich through crime. The lives of the criminals were a disaster. They lived in fear, paranoia, and distrust. I had a rich grandfather and a poor grandfather. The rich one, had property because he had a successful business for many years. I began to realize as a teenager, that crime did not pay very well at all, being in your own business did.

One night there were about seven people in our pickup truck, three in the cab and four in the bed of the truck. We were driving across town when a car pulls up behind the truck.

The guy driving the car had tried to crash a party we had, days earlier. There had been a fight at the party. During the fight, I had tried to pull this guy out of his car holding him by his hair. They wanted to crash our party and we would not let them, so they got mad and started threatening us. A fight ensued.

Now, these same people were following us. We saw them pull out a shotgun, pointing it at our truck. We began to swerve and speed off as they started shooting. Thank God, they missed. Disaster averted. Now there had to be payback.

Few days later we were told where these people were. Two of my family got so angry and got some guns to go after them. After all, they shot at our friends and us.

We devised a plan. We suckered them into following us, before they could start shooting at us, one person that had been laying down in the bed of the truck stood up and started firing into the car. The radiator, the hood, and windshield had holes in them and one person got shot.

We were arrested later that night, but because of connections and some threats, all charges were dropped.

A few days later, I am alone driving down the street. I

see these same people in another car coming up behind me. I see they have a shotgun or a rifle, getting ready to aim it from inside the car, so they can shoot me. The street came to a dead end. I would have to turn left or right. I knew if I turned, they would start shooting.

So as soon as I turned I floored it and started burning rubber, to get away as fast as I could and then turned down another street. One tire was shot out and bullet holes filled the sides of the truck. One would have gone into my heart if it had been two inches higher. I could have died.

Some of my family and friends loved fights and violence. I don't. I liked excitement but not fighting or violence but that was part of my life.

At 17, when my stepfather died from a heart attack, we had his funeral and obviously went to the cemetery. Now my stepfather was a functioning alcoholic. His brother blamed me, for some reason, for the death of Charlie, his brother and my stepfather.

The following happened we guessed, because my stepbrother David, told my stepfather and his brother, some things that I had supposedly done. My stepbrother was afraid of my friends, my family and me. We had him convinced we were tied to serious organized crime, so he would be scared, and would not tell the police or anyone what we were doing.

My stepfather's brother, at about 40 years of age, wanted to get revenge on me and decided to attack me, physically beating me up. He was probably 6 feet 4 and weighed about 240 lbs. I was about 155lbs and was 5 ft 10. Right after the burial of my stepfather at the cemetery, my half-brother Keith overheard the plan that was being whispered and being set into motion. Charlie's brother said something like, "I am going over there to kill him with my bare hands" or something similar. Charlie's brother was talking about killing me.

Now a new plan was immediately devised and set in motion. So instead of him attacking me, my close family and friends confronted him. He then began to run, when he saw he was not just up against a 17-year-old kid, that weighed 150 lbs., but against a family that was supporting me. We, my brothers, my friends and I, literally chased him and his family out of town.

I was in a car with my grandfather, JW, two or three cars were filled with my family and friends defending me, by chasing him and his family out of town. We drove 90 to 100 mph down US Highway 80, chasing them out of town. If he had stopped or tried to fight me, as he said he was going to do, he would have been very sorry he ever messed with me. He was not afraid of me; it was my family and friends. We never saw that side of the family again. It was times like this that I valued my friends and family. This was my life. Of course, much of my family had no clue what was going on. They were naïve and did not want to know what was going on. This was my life.

One night we held a family meeting, my brothers, cousins, an aunt, an uncle, and my mother were present. It was a "legal strategy" meeting on how to deal with criminal charges that would later be dropped. When my aunt left, she called and said she saw they were being followed as they left the house. She said the police will probably be following everyone as they leave, so be careful. They were watching us at the meeting.

This was my life as a teenager.

CHAPTER III

OUT OF DARKNESS

Almost every Friday and Saturday night, we would be at clubs drinking and partying. It was not uncommon for a fight to ensue inside the club or even outside. Often one of us would be in a fight. Occasionally it would be a free for all fight, people pulled across tables, and fights spilling onto the dance floor. Rednecks and alcohol usually meant fights. My family and friends were pretty much redneck, good ole boys, if you understand what I mean.

So, one Saturday night we were at a different bar drinking and talking. My sister in law and another woman got into a fight. Rednecks always liked to watch two girls fight. The fight went from inside the bar to the parking lot. The two women were rolling around fighting on top of the sidewalk and the parking lot. They were hitting, pulling hair, and everything else that goes on in a girl fight. I was just there minding on own business and watching the fight. Unexpectedly, this guy hits me three times before I even realized I am in a fight. Now I am in a fight for my life.

I had a lot of leg strength, but I was more of a wrestler than a boxer. My legs were so strong that one time a car we were in, spun out on the highway. It ended up on a 45-degree incline to the side of the highway, with the front of the car facing down. There were these wood posts about 8 inches' diameter in the ground about one foot in front of the car. The angle was too great, making it impossible to get back up to the highway. There were these wood posts in the ground surrounding the park. I thought to myself if I could just pull the post out of the ground with my hands, using my legs as leverage, we could drive out of the park. So, that was what I did. I reached down and pulled the 8-inch diameter post out of the ground with my two hands. So, you could say I was strong.

So back at the club, the guy started punching me. He was very fast with his punches, but luckily, his punches were not very powerful. The fight was on. Somehow I knocked him down and he ended up under a car. Then he got out on the other side. Three times, he tried to take me out but could not. I was like a Timex watch it "Takes a licking and keeps on ticking." He kept coming, but I would not quit. He was too fast for me. But when I got him down he would get away.

My half-brother saw us fighting and stepped up to my defense. The fight began to expand. Now there were about 15 people against the two of us. Fists were flying. I did not even know who I was fighting some of the time. Yet through it all, they did not win, but neither did we. Then one of them pulled out a gun. Which is when we left.

The guy that attacked me put out his hand to shake my hand as a sign of respect. He respected me because he could not beat me. I wanted nothing to do with it. I hated fighting and I sure did not want to be his friend, after the fight.

I found out later this was one of the best street fighters in the entire north and eastern region of Texas and everyone that knew him, was afraid of him. I did not care who he was or his reputation. I wanted to get even. He tore up my clothes and I had bruises and cuts all over my body from this fight.

Two days later I was at a kitchen table and a friend of mine saw what had happened to me. He said I can get you some dynamite, so you can blow up the club, kill the guy and get even. This is how my friends thought.

At about the same time a family member told my grandmother what had happened to me. She and my mother were afraid of what the consequences would be for the guys, that did this. They knew revenge would be coming.

My Grandmother, Thelma was a Christian and quoted the verse of the Bible about vengeance belongs unto the Lord and "He will repay". I thought yeah right. She said let God take care of it.

For the first time in my life I thought OK God, I am going to prove you and see if you are for real. I said, "God if you are real, you deal with this guy". I talked the family out of taking revenge. No one had any idea why. I wanted to see if vengeance did belong to the Lord.

A few months later the man that attacked me was killed. He was killed at a club in Houston, Texas, hundreds of miles from us. None of us had anything to do with his death. This was my first wake up call, that God was trying to get through to me. God was trying to show me he wanted a relationship with me. I thought OK, was that a coincidence, or was it God taking care of it for me.

I would later see many people trying to stop me or stop what I was doing, die. God would fight many battles for me and people would die that attacked me, in one form or other in the future.

The reality that there was a God and the supernatural might be real, began to dawn on my consciousness. I ran across a book about white magic and other books that showed how to walk in some supernatural things, per ancient manuscripts such as pyramid power, pendulum power, star of the east, auras, astral projection and the like. I began to realize a lot of people had supernatural experiences, some with God, but many without God. But I saw there were clearly supernatural experiences to be had.

I had experienced so many things. I had lots of excitement, lots of adventures, experiences of so many kinds but I never had a supernatural experience. I wanted a supernatural experience. I had already become disillusioned with what life had to offer and was looking for something. I had no idea what.

The first "supernatural" experience happened with pendulum power. You put a crystal or stone on the end of a string and ask questions. It swings one way for yes, the other direction for no. To my surprise, I was holding a stone on the end of a string and asked a question from a spirit that might be around. The stone started moving all by itself. Eventually, it was moving violently in the direction of yes or no for anything I would ask.

I then asked," Is there a god?". The answer was yes. I asked if there is a devil? The answer was yes. I asked, "Is this from the devil or God. It began to swing violently in the direction of the Devil. It was replying this was from the devil.

This scared me. I had been raised a Baptist. I did not want to be doing something with the Devil. The spirit himself answered me that it was from the Devil. Wow. This was my first supernatural experience. It defied logic. But I experienced it. I never expected my first supernatural experience was with the Devil instead of God. My mind and my heart were going in so many directions because of this experience.

I later learned from quantum theory that the mind itself could cause things to move. I used this pendulum power for betting on horse races and discovered it was not very accurate. So, I decided even though it is something that defies logic, and appears supernatural, it cannot be trusted. If it was something supernatural I wanted it to be real and to have the right answer every time.

One day my mother came in and said here is a little book someone gave me at a health food store. You might want to read it.

I said what is it about. She said I don't know, the name of it is," The Game of Life and How to Play it". I thought that sounds interesting. I always wanted to know how to play the game of life.

As I began to read this little book, there were stories after stories, of personal experiences, where people experienced all kinds of amazing miracles and healings from God. It said God was looking for faith and when God sees your faith, he then does miracles on your behalf.

This was the first time anyone ever told me about faith and how faith worked. I realized the message of faith is what I was missing as a kid, looking to have an experience with God. I was told accept it by faith, but no one explained what faith was or that you could see actions of faith, or that there were many examples of faith, causing God to work in your behalf, in the Bible.

When I heard this message of faith in God and towards God, in my heart, I knew that this was right, and was what I had been missing my whole life. I knew faith was at the heart of experiencing God. I realized that through faith you could have an experience with God, and have God working in your life. I thought wow! Why have I never heard of this before?

At the end of the book, that was the little prayer that I prayed.

I prayed, "Lord Jesus come into my heart and forgive me of my sin". When I prayed that prayer, it felt like 10,000 lbs. was lifted off my shoulders. It was amazing. I prayed that prayer before, many times but it was never in faith, so nothing happened. I had never felt anything like it.

I knew I was forgiven. I knew Jesus had shown himself alive and was real to me. I knew this was my first real experience with the Lord Jesus Christ and it was because of faith. It was what I sought for years earlier but never experienced. Yet it was the first experience of many to come.

CHAPTER IV

EXPERIENCES OF A NEW BELIEVER

Some of the experiences I am about to share with you may seem unimaginable, some of these experiences you will read about, may seem completely foreign to you, they were to me. You may be like me and may have not even known of anyone ever experiencing these things before. I had never even heard of these things before, so I understand. So, keep an open mind and heart as I did. These stories are all true and I believed happened because my heart was totally open to the Lord. I wanted to learn and have more experiences with a true living God. I also wanted to relive that feeling of fresh forgiveness and the presence of God.

After my initial conversion experience, I was told to do three things. I was told to pray for others. I was also told to read the Bible every day and at least one chapter of Proverbs every day. I was also told to do a sin list, writing down everything I had ever done, asking the Lord to forgive me and to cleanse me from it. I was told after I did the sin list, I should burn it, to show myself, as a sign to myself, that God will remember my sins no more and he has forgotten them. Just as sin written on paper and burned, can no longer be found, so sin forgiven by God, is utterly totally forgiven and wiped out. So, I did what

I was told, I could easily go back and feel that joy of fresh forgiveness almost any time.

A few weeks later I had written down a prayer list, for lots of people that needed to get saved and some other prayer requests. Every night I would pray over these before I went to bed. It was always on the nightstand beside the bed.

One morning when I woke up it was gone. The paper I had written on, with the names of people I was praying for, vanished. We looked everywhere for it and it never showed up anywhere. Years later when the house was sold, and the furniture moved out, I looked to see if the paper was anywhere to be found. I never found it. I sensed God caused it to disappear to boost my faith that he heard and saw my prayers and would answer them.

The next experience happened because of reading the Bible. As I was reading my Bible I began to read John14:12. Being raised a Baptist I was always taught to believe the Bible, if you ever must make a choice between believing a man or the Bible, believe the Bible. You might not understand something, but you should believe it is true. So, after reading this passage that said if I believed on Jesus, the works he did, I would do also. I was shocked.

I thought, "You mean I am to do the works of Jesus, the same miracles he did, I am supposed to be doing?" Wow. I read this phrase many times. I read it in context. The context was clearly miracles. I had never seen a miracle or had even heard of a miracle happening anywhere, other than in books. To think God wanted to and expected to do miracles through me. I couldn't believe the Bible said this. Yet it was so clear. To me at first, it was just unbelievable.

I had a dilemma, either believe the Bible, that said I would do the works of Jesus or not believe the Bible. I knew Jesus was real. I had felt the forgiveness and the presence of God.

I knew Jesus and his forgiveness was real. But was the Bible truly God's word to man.

I earnestly prayed as sincere as I could. "I know that YOU are real, I hope the Bible is real and true, because if not, how do I know how to live my life. If the Bible isn't true and I won't do the works of Jesus, take my life now, for my life is not worth living if the Bible isn't true". I prayed this many ways from my heart. This was to be a turning point, an epiphany.

I honestly preferred to be dead, rather than to live a life with the Lord, knowing the Bible was false and could not be trusted. I knew Jesus was real but was the Bible something I could trust? I was so sincere, willing to die, and wanting to die, if the Bible was not true and not in fact, God's word to man.

I needed something to give me the direction I needed to live. I knew I needed direction and guidance. If the Bible was not true, but Jesus was real, where would I get the direction and guidance I needed to live and be happy.

Something happened that day. I can't say what happened, but I know something happened inside of me. It was like there was now a sense of destiny that I would do the works of Jesus. I knew I was destined for the miraculous and to see healings and miracles.

A few weeks later My mother gave me a book about casting out devils or demons called "Pigs in the Parlor" by Frank Hammond. Frank Hammond's brother played the organ at First Baptist Church in Terrell my hometown and had even taught me piano lessons. I thought to myself this must be the most boring book if Mr. Hammond's brother wrote it. Then I started reading it.

My mother asked me about it and I began to read some of it out loud to her. We both were mesmerized, by what I was reading. It was about people that had demons or evil spirits in them, making them do things and tormenting them. It showed from the Bible where Jesus cast out devils. The book stated these spirits where still here in the earth. Frank and his wife would cast these spirits out of demon oppressed people and they would have freedom from addictions and bad habits, once they were delivered.

I remembered two people in my life, VW and the assaulter that had attacked me. They probably had demon spirits or devils in them causing these things. I read where Jesus cast these devils out of people. I knew the eyes I had seen years earlier was probably the eyes, of one possessed of a devil, to have sex. This explained a lot.

As I was reading this book out loud, the metal mobile home roof we were living in, began making loud noises, but there was no wind. There were popping and squeaking sounds, from where we did not know.

My mother and I, both were scared. We knew it must be spirits or devils, like the ones we were reading about. We both tried to cast out the spirits from the house and each other. We were trying anything to get rid of them.

Right after the noises started, I looked at my mother and she looked like some form of wolf. She said she looked at me, I had bright red rings, around my eyelids. We were quoting scriptures that were in the book, and the noise eventually stopped.

We were so scared we took everything out of the house that the book said created ties to anything demonic. We even took out all the alcoholic beverages and poured them out in the fire as well. The fire shot up and made a very weird looking flame. It looked almost like a spirit body made of fire. This scared us more.

We now had an experience with spirits or demons or

devils. I tried to cast them out of my mother, she tried to cast them out of me. This book said most people had some type of demon spirit oppressing them and needed deliverance. So, we did everything they said in the book.

One day after I commanded the spirit to leave my mother, her eye sight was perfect, and she did not even need glasses. We both were shocked and impressed by this. Was sickness caused, at least sometimes, by spirits or devils?

This book made me so demon conscious and so focused on demons that within a couple of weeks of trying to cast out devils, I was tired of it. I was frustrated. I did not know if I had a demon spirit in me or not.

Without a doubt, I had an amazing experience that night. I knew there had been real demonic activity in and around the house, when we were reading that book. I knew I had done a lot of bad things, that might have opened the door to the devil in my life.

One night out of desperation, I cried out to the Lord. I said, I don't know if I have any devils in me or not, but if I do, deliver me now". Right after this prayer of desperation, I started to cough a little bit, not much and coughed up a wad of blood. After I washed my mouth from the blood there was no more problem as far as bleeding or any source of blood.

The book had said sometimes when God delivers someone from a spirit they cough up blood. I thought about the book, the Lord apparently delivered me from a spirit, that had been in my life.

Over the years, the Lord would teach me many things about dealing with spirits and devils but this was my first experience. I would not recommend *Pigs in the Parlor* as a source book for dealing properly with the devil and spirits, but it opened me up to a new experience with God. Now I knew experientially, that God was my deliverer. I cried out to the

Lord and he delivered me.

The next book I read was *Praise Avenue* by Don Gossett. This book taught me the importance of praising God and how praise could change your life. After reading the book, I began to praise God for two or three hours at a time, several days a week. Any time that I needed to feel the presence of God, I would just start praising the Lord. I would start praising God and within thirty minutes to an hour I usually would feel the joy of the Lord, rise in me and I would experience the presence of God.

It was wonderful to be able to experience the Lord, anytime I would worship and praise him for more than 2 hours. I knew only a few songs, so I would make up songs, or just sing whatever came into my mind to the Lord. At first it was difficult, but when I started experiencing joy unspeakable, and the presence of God. It eventually became easy. I loved to experience the Lord in worship and praise.

I was still an undercover Christian. I did not tell people I was a Christian. I knew I wasn't strong enough to withstand the pressure. I just avoided a lot of my bad influence friends. One day I was talking to my half-brother and his wife. They told me about a guaranteed money jewel robbery in Oklahoma. I was told they were putting together a team and wanted me to be a part of the team. The fix was in, everything was set. It was just pulling it off. I was by this time 20.

Years earlier I told myself, I would not do anything criminal, unless the payoff would be potentially worth the prison time. I think the devil knew this, and knew I liked excitement. I had always wanted to be a high-end jewel thief, like in the movies. It seemed so cool. This was to steal $100,000 worth of jewelry. The fence and everything was set. What would I do?

I knew I couldn't do it, because now I am a Christian. I

could not tell them this is the reason for not wanting to do it, for I was afraid. I was afraid to tell them about my experience or being a Christian now. So, I start poking holes in their plan. I start with saying, this is across state lines, so this would be a federal case and the FBI would be involved in this, if it ever came back to us. I knew they were afraid of the FBI and it worked. That combined with my questions about who had the fix in, shook their confidence in doing this easy job. So, I was out of it. Thank God.

Not long after this experience I began to hear a lot about the "Baptism of the Holy Spirit". Being raised as a Baptist, I thought baptism of the Holy Spirit happened in water baptism. But this was completely different.

Father Dennis Bennett, an Episcopal priest, began to teach about this Holy Spirit baptism, and showed lots of scripture regarding a baptism of the Holy Spirit that came with power. I knew I did not have the power I needed. I saw in the Bible (Acts 1:8) that you shall receive power, when the Holy Spirit comes upon you.

The experience with demon spirits taught me I needed power. I knew I was still an undercover Christian and knew I needed power. I did not even have the power to tell my experiences. Father Dennis Bennett taught me a lot of things regarding the Holy Spirit, that was in the Bible.

In the book of Acts every Christian that received the Holy Spirit, immediately or eventually, spoke in tongues. I decided I wanted this Baptism of the Holy Spirit and power experience, yet I did not want the tongues, but apparently, it was a package deal. They came together.

I was so afraid of tongues, as a Baptist boy, I was told it was of the devil. Yet this Episcopal priest had this experience and these people in the Bible did as well. I decided yes, I want this, despite my fear. I wanted this other experience with God, that apparently was waiting for every believer in Jesus Christ. This experience that would bring power into my life.

I was taught the first thing to do, was to ask for the Baptism of the Holy Spirit. To be honest I was very nervous. I did not know what to expect. I asked Jesus to baptize me with the Holy Spirit, and to give me the evidence of speaking in tongues.

In the Bible, it said The Holy Spirit joins with us, whereby we cry "Abba" to the Lord. "Abba" means "Daddy or Papa" but it is also a foreign tongue or language to me. So, I would then pray Abba, Abba.

I wanted to be able to pray the perfect prayer for anything, as the Holy Spirit gave the inspiration, in a language I did not know, so I could not mess it up. This was a great gift, a prayer language that gave an ability to pray the perfect prayer, a prayer in the perfect will of God. A prayer that was not dependent on me or my knowledge but a "grace prayer". Even as the Bible calls the Holy Spirit, the Spirit of Grace and Prayer.

Every night I prayed for this, I was very nervous. I did not know what feelings I would have, or exactly what I would experience. What would I feel? What would this experience with the Holy Spirit be like? Some of the experiences people had in the Bible with the Holy Spirit were awesome. There was wind blowing, ground shaking, tongues of fire falling... Of course, some were quiet and not dramatic. Of course, I wanted the dramatic.

So, I earnestly prayed for Jesus to baptize me in the Holy Spirit and then spoke "Abba, Abba". Each night some little syllables would come into my mind like fa, sa, da or something similar. I did this for three nights.

The next day I was down at my "rich" grandfather's house, repairing his shower. He now had very little money, but he did have houses and a lot of property. The shower floor had fallen through, and my grandfather always used the shower. They had another bathroom, but I wanted to repair the shower, so my grandfather could have his shower back. They did not have the extra money to do this, so I decided to do it, and pay for it, myself. I had to tear things out and get a shower pan and install it. Disconnect drains and install new ones. It was a lot of work. I even decided to put a seat in the shower, so he could sit in the shower, since he was getting elderly.

I was out in the garage alone, working, cutting some material for the shower. I was just humming or singing some songs to myself.

Suddenly, I heard myself singing in tongues, the gift of tongues in song form. Wow! I was so excited; this was so great. I experienced singing in tongues, the gift from the Holy Spirit. Later I started speaking in tongues.

From that experience forward, I immediately stopped cussing, yet it was not me, but the Holy Spirit in me, without any real effort on my part. I used to cuss a lot, and from the moment I sang in tongues, it all stopped. It wasn't me stopping it. It was completely grace and the Holy Spirit. Now decades later I still never cuss.

I had been growing as a believer but took a job in Florida with my uncle Phil, so I wasn't around any of the bad influences in my life, which was a good thing.

I stayed at a friend of my uncle's house. We were there doing a remodel project and stayed in one of their houses. They had a small library in the house and I found a book called "Healing Everywhere" by an Episcopal priest, John Banks. I guess it was the first book, just about healing that I ever read. It was amazing to me, to be reading about all the people getting healed.

I was watching Pat Robertson on CBN one night and he said I want to ask you a question. What stands out to you most about Jesus ministry? He said how you answer that, will show you where you are at and probably what your ministry is.

I thought everyone will say healing. So, I began to ask people that question. To my amazement almost no one said his healings

People said his love, his teaching and many other things. But all non-Christians always said his death on the cross. I then realized non-Christians first had to see the cross. After you were a Christian the focus, then began to be on your ministry, or what Jesus had called you personally to. I thought, does God want me to have a healing ministry?

After 9 months from the time I prayed to receive Christ and be forgiven, I still did not have a church home. After I read John 14:12 I looked for a church that believed and preached John 14:12. I knew the Baptist did not believe that believers were supposed to do the works and miracles of Jesus. I was afraid to go to a Pentecostal church, because I was told as a Baptist boy, they were of the Devil. I later learned this wasn't true, but as a new believer, I did not want to take a chance of going to a church that was of the devil.

When I returned from Florida I knew I needed to find a church. One Friday night at 10:30 pm there was a 30-minute service from a Dallas church. I saw this minister Bob, from a church called Word of Faith on the TV. He was preaching everything God had been showing me. I was so excited, I finally found someone that agreed with what God had shown me from the Bible.

So, I decided to visit this church in Farmers Branch, Texas. When we came in the doors of the church it was electric. The praise and worship were so good. You could feel the power and presence of God, like I had never experienced before. I knew this was to be my church home.

The church was meeting in a converted warehouse and

had concrete floors. It was not very pretty, but wow the service was great. Everything from the worship, to the preaching, was the best experience I had ever had in a church.

The church was about 45 miles away from where I lived. I needed a new vehicle, if I was going to be driving to church, every Sunday morning, Sunday evening and Wednesday nights. I said Lord if you want me to go to this church, you need to help me get a new truck. I had just been turned down from a new truck loan, because I had no credit. I did not even have a credit card. That next week, my uncle suggested I go to Rockwall Ford, to a salesman that was a friend of the family, for many decades. So, I went there and bought a truck that was much, much better than the first truck I tried to buy. It was a top of the line Ford Lariat and the payments were even cheaper. Wow! Now I could go to church easily and in style.

After I got this truck I would be going to church every time there was any kind of meeting. Church was so good, I loved it and my new pastor, Pastor Bob. He could be so funny, especially on the Sunday night services. Sunday night was my favorite service. Then Pastor Bob was just being himself and he felt free to just be led by the Holy Spirit. Some of those Sunday night services I still remember, they were so powerful.

Some weeks I would drive about 600 miles to go to 6 church services a week, but most weeks only about 300 miles. I would be taking family and friends with me, to church, as well as going to other Bible studies and on many Tuesday nights, meetings at Christ for the Nations Institute. At CFNI they had guest speakers come in and speak. I was hungry for God and hungry to learn.

CHAPTER V

THE CALL FOR SERVICE

I had prayed to receive Christ several years earlier, so I wasn't expecting a life changing experience. As I drove along the freeway, going to church, the Lord spoke to me saying "Tonight you will make a decision that will change your life". I went on to the church and met my father and stepmother, whom I had invited to church that night. I usually sat at the front of the church, but I sat towards the back, to sit with my father.

The service went along about the same as always. I enjoyed the praise, worship, and the Word that night. At the end of the message I thought, "I wonder what is going to happen tonight". Then Pastor Bob started giving an altar call for salvation. My heart started pounding inside of me. I felt the Spirit of the Lord all over me in a very powerful, unique way. As the altar call continued, I was ready to say yes to anything that God wanted me to do.

I thought what is happening? I know I am saved. I have no doubt about that, yet my heart was pounding within me. It was immediately after this that Pastor Bob said, "since the church was started, I have never done this, but God is really dealing with someone very strongly, because he has called you to the ministry".

I knew he was talking about me, so I immediately went to the altar. I immediately knew that this was the decision that the Lord was talking to me about a few hours earlier. Pastor Bob then laid his hands upon me. There was no one behind me to catch me, for no one expected me to fall to the ground under the power of the Holy Spirit. But as Brother Bob laid his hands upon me, I fell to the ground.

The church at that time was meeting in a converted warehouse. The floors were painted concrete. So, when I fell to the ground, immediately I felt my bones hit the concrete. By the time my head hit the concrete, I felt no pain, only the presence of the Lord. In the natural, I would have been seriously hurt, by a fall like that, but this was of the Holy Spirit, overcome by the power of God.

The Lord tried to show me from the beginning of the call to the ministry that it would only be by his power and might that I would be able to fulfill the call of God. Without him, his power, grace and gifting, I would end up a pile of hurting, broken bones.

The next week I drove from the Dallas area, where my home was, to Houston for a construction job that my uncle and I had going there.

I always enjoyed the weekends in Houston when I was there, because I would then go to Brother John Osteen's Lakewood Church.

But this week I was amazed at what happened as I read my Bible. I began to see so many things in the scripture I had never seen before. Every time I opened the Bible I would get a new revelation from the Lord. After receiving the call and the anointing for ministry, I was receiving more revelation from God than I had ever even thought possible. It was so wonderful.

I had been taught about the impartation of the Holy Spirit and gifts through the laying on of hands. So, I realized this gift must have been imparted to me by Pastor Bob, the Sunday night before. I was so amazed at the revelation of the Bible that the call and the grace for ministry brought forth. I had been diligent to read and study the Bible before this, but now my eyes were open in way they had never been before. This grace and inspiration of the Holy Spirit was so strong, that I began to learn things that were clearly in the Bible, I just had never seen it. God had truly opened my eyes to see, and my heart to understand. The Lord had caused the Word of God to really become the living, alive, powerful relevant Word for today. This would become the cornerstone of my ministry, teaching God's word.

As I would later learn, the ministry would require more than just being called of God and having the inspiration of the Holy Spirit. The ministry would require a total commitment that at times would have my life at stake.

CHAPTER VI

THE 102-YEAR-OLD LADY

After the call to ministry I started pastoring a small church in Terrell. There were not many people or things to do, so I started ministering in four nursing homes as often as weekly. Two of the nursing homes were normal and had very typical responses to messages and the singing we had, that was like a short church service.

Two of these nursing homes were very different. One man at Rosehill would be beating his head against his chair that he was tied into. He would scream unintelligible sounds every time I would start to preach. At Locust Grove, every time we would start singing, this one man would start slithering down the aisle on the floor. Another sweet lady resident had been born with three eyes.

These were my first experiences in ministry. I was praying Lord, teach me how to deal with these things properly. I was feeling a little overwhelmed with these strange realities when I met someone interesting. I was on my rounds, greeting the residents when I met a black lady that was bedfast and legally blind but influenced my life greatly.

This lady had been an itinerant healing evangelist in the

1920's. She would go from town to town as the Lord would lead her. She would preach, lead people to the Lord and pray for people to get healed. She saw many great miracles, and many come to an experience with the Lord Jesus Christ.

She had been born just after the civil war. She would tell me stories of what it was like during those times. It was very hard times with extreme poverty, for almost all former slaves in the south. Many people rejected her because she was a Christian, others rejected her for preaching healing, others mocked her for believing in speaking in tongues. Many shunned her because she was a woman preacher and many because she was black. But she persevered through it all.

Eventually she married a Church of God in Christ preacher where she and her husband served as Pastors until he died. She was now legally blind and bedfast.

The amazing thing about her was not just her story, but her present experiences she was having with God. I would come in and ask her, "How are you doing?" and she would start telling me her experiences that week.

Sometimes she would speak of Heaven and the beauty of Heaven and how loving her Lord Jesus was. Quite often she would speak of visions of the heavenly and earthly.

As she would pray in the spirit and the Lord would take her to Africa, to villages she was interceding for. She would tell me about the people in her visions and what she thought it meant.

Oftentimes I would come in and she would tell me about our church service that previous Sunday morning. Physically she wasn't there, but she could tell you about it spiritually. She would say something like, "Oh the worship was so sweet in your service Sunday". As she would pray the Lord would show her the service. She was not there physically but was there spiritually.

I was amazed that a 102-year-old lady that was legally blind, bedfast and could not even sit up most days, could still be impacting the world from her bed. Through the Holy Spirit and praying in the spirit, she was praying for different people around the world from her hospital bed in a nursing home in Terrell, Texas. Her reach was not limited by her physical body or physical abilities. As long as she prayed, she could not be held to one place, her mind and spirit would visit places around the world. I know because she told me about her experiences very often.

At first, I was skeptical about them, thinking they were delusions, but when she would tell me about our church services, about myself and would try to encourage me, I eventually became a believer.

I often wonder if my trips to Africa and other places, came because of this lady praying and interceding for me. Many of the things she told me about, I saw when I went to Africa.

This woman never stopped serving the Lord, even though she became blind and could not even get out of bed. She was still a person of influence, possibly one of the greatest persons of influence I would ever meet. Being blind, bedfast and black did not stop her. How could I complain about anything, knowing what she went through?

CHAPTER VII

MIRACLES OF PROVISION

Along the way of life, God will often prepare people for service in many unusual ways. God sometimes probably smiled as he saw me trying to walk in faith and obedience. Every miracle I saw and experienced was a foundation for more miracles, further down the road of life. This chapter will tell of a couple of miracles, signs or wonders that the Lord did which helped prepare me to be able to accomplish what others had been unable to do, years later in Sierra Leone, West Africa. Most of the miracles I have seen, happened merely because I was trying to obey God and follow him.

One of the first miracles I experienced was a miracle of provision. I had been driving 45 miles one way to church on Sunday morning, Sunday night, Wednesday night, and special meetings. So, one day, as I was going to church, I started talking to the Lord. I said Lord; you need to do something for me, after all I have been doing a lot for you lately. Immediately after I said this to the Lord, I looked at my gas gauge. The gas gauge was on empty. I thought, well I need to stop and get some gas. I was working and had money, so I was completely surprised at what began to happen. As I looked at the gas gauge, the Lord started filling my gas tank with gas. It went from empty, and steadily went up. I was shocked. At first I thought something happened to my gas gauge, but then I knew God had performed a miracle. I wasn't concerned about the gas, after all I had plenty of money. I was just glad that the Lord had shown himself alive and powerful to me.

Several years later the Lord spoke to me to go visit my father, who lived about 70 miles from where I lived. I was trying to do the work of the ministry and had almost no money. Yet I knew the Lord spoke to me and said to go visit my father. So, I went out of the house and started the car that Celia Bonds, a missionary to France, had left with me while she was in France. As I started the car, I saw there was less than one-fourth of a tank of gas. Well I figured that if the Lord blessed the gas I would make it to my father's house without running out of gas.

My father was now a Christian and would sometimes give me some money to help me in the ministry. Therefore, I thought the Lord would use my father to give me some money for gas. I ate dinner with my father and stepmother. We talked and had an enjoyable time. It was getting late, so I decided I had better leave. I thought, "Well, my father will offer to give me some money as I go out of the door". As I left the house I realized he wasn't going to be giving me any money.

When I left the house, I had less than one dollar, which is what I had when I came. I thought about what I could do. I could go and ask my dad for some money, or I could believe God. I said, "Lord, you told me to visit my father, you told me to come here. Therefore, Lord, you must provide". My father didn't invite me, the Lord told me to go, so he would have to be responsible and provide the gas.

As I started the car to leave, the gas gauge was well below empty. I knew I had to have a miracle or I would run out of gas quickly within a mile or two. I knew the Lord had told me to go. I didn't want to be embarrassed in my attempt to obey God. After all, my father didn't tell me to come, my heavenly Father did. Therefore, the responsibility would be on my heavenly Father to provide.

I knew I wasn't in faith. I knew I needed the gift of the working of miracles, in addition to the gift of faith, so I began seeking the gifts of the Holy Spirit.

I kept saying over and over "Lord, I thank you for the gift of the working of miracles, putting gas in this car. Lord, I thank you for the gift of faith and the working of miracles. Holy Spirit, I thank you for the working of miracles, I thank you for putting gas in the car." I kept saying this over and over as I started driving home. I knew faith required action, so my action of faith was to drive home while the gas gauge was on empty. When I arrived home, there was one-fourth of a tank of gas in the car. This was the amount I had when I left the house. God had truly worked a miracle.

These miracles are what probably gave me the courage to step out in faith, many times in the future.

CHAPTER VIII

THE FRENCH CONNECTION

My first missionary journey would be to Paris, France. I knew God wanted me to start ministering in other countries. but I had no invitations to go anywhere.   One Friday night I was in a meeting and a woman named Rev. Loraine Gross began to prophesy to me, saying that I would receive a letter of invitation to go somewhere within 10 days, and that I was to accept it.

I was eagerly waiting to see what would happen within 10 days. Just as prophesied, I received a letter from Celia Bonds for me to come to Paris, France and help in the work there.   I later had a dream about when I was to go as well.

I had told some people that I was to go to France I believe it was September 30, 1983. I knew it was the will of God, but I didn't have any money to go. I thought surely God will speak to someone and will pay for my ticket there, after all it wasn't like I was going to get paid or anything. So, I waited on God. But nothing happened.

The day came and went, but no money.

The next day I was upset with God. I decided not to go to church that evening, after all I was mad at God for letting me down.

I decided to pray during the time I would normally be at church. While I was praying, the Lord spoke to me that I wasn't really committed to going. I said, Lord what do you mean? He showed me how that I could make one phone call and make about $800 – $1000 in one week, for a little remodel contract. That would give me enough money for the ticket there. So, I said, OK Lord I will do it". So, I made the call got the little job and then had the money to go. At the same time as I made the call something else happened.

My mother saw a friend of mine at church. He was a businessman named Tim Shreve, who is now a missionary in Sweden. He asked my mother if I had received the money to go to France. She said "no, but we know that God will provide it". Tim said, well the Lord spoke to me to give $1000 to help pay for Kyle's tickets. My mother rejoiced as Tim wrote out a check for $1000. That night my mother brought the check to me.

Once I was committed to do what it took to go, then God moved to help me have the money I needed to go. Within two weeks I was in Europe.

When I arrived in Paris, France at Orly Airport, no one was there to meet me, for they had all gone to Germany. After all I was 2 weeks late from the date the Lord had said. I was alone in a foreign country, not knowing what to do and not knowing where to go.

I immediately went to a hotel and started praying and fasting. At the end of three days, I felt a release in my spirit, or a witness in my spirit, that God had taken care of the situation. Within 30 minutes of the witness in my spirit, I was finally able to contact some people in France and Germany.

I left the hotel and was on my way to Germany within 30 minutes of having that victory, release, or witness in my spirit.

Before the witness in my spirit I had called and tried to contact some people, but it all came to nothing. Afterwards it was so easy.

The first miracle was getting to Gare de L'est train station, from the hotel near Orly Airport. Taxis in Europe were very expensive, so I immediately dismissed taking a taxi. I had never been on a train or subway system, after all I was redneck from Texas. So, it would all be a totally new experience for me.

Honestly, I was quite nervous and scared. This was the first time I had been overseas and really followed the Lord out of my comfort zone.

I took a bus from the hotel to a subway station. When I saw, the SNCF train station sign. I thought, this is the train station, this is so easy. After I purchased my train ticket to Germany, I discovered this was just a sales office in the subway station. I felt so stupid.

Since I didn't speak French, I didn't understand what to do or where to go. The only thing I knew was that I had to do something.

My Pastor had always said do something, lest you do nothing. So, I got on the Metro subway train. I didn't know where I was, or where I was going. After some time, I thought I needed to get off the train. So, I got off the subway train.

I asked several people, but no one understood English.

Again, I thought I must do something, so I got on another subway train. After I was on this train for a while I looked up and saw we had just arrived at Gare de L'est. Unknowingly, I had taken the most direct route possible to get to the train station.

I had no idea where I was going, but God directed my steps. I experienced being led by an Angel of God, while nervous and afraid, in the middle of my confusion. I had no idea I was being led by God, yet I was.

When I arrived in Germany, it was the day before the "Americans for Jesus Rally" was to start. I immediately offered my services and began helping Major Tom Demont, and the others that helped organize this meeting. Vicki Jamison Peterson was the keynote speaker as well as others from the states. I could help with the meetings, do the sound, help set up equipment as well as minister, at the military base in Augsburg, Germany.

There were several interesting experiences that happened in Augsburg. There were probably 15 people staying at Major Demont's house, on the base in Germany during these meetings. Pastor John Stitt and I were rooming together in the basement, so we decided to have a time praying and interceding in the Spirit.

Well without realizing it, we had gotten so loud in our praying, we had woken up everyone in the house. I had my eyes closed praying out loud in the Spirit, when suddenly I felt a hand come across my mouth. It was Celia. Not very many in the house appreciated our zeal for the Lord in praying. So, we apologized and quieted down.

I was helping in the meetings from about 8-9 in the morning until about 10 every night. So, I would be praying in tongues quietly, almost the whole time I was working the sound, or during the messages. One morning I shared with the people that I felt we really needed to pray for the meetings. Vicki Jamison Peterson was there. That night she asked everyone to really pray for the meetings, so the people did.

A couple of nights later Vicki felt the leading of the Lord to take up the main offering to meet the budget a day early. The push to raise the budget was planned to be done the last night of the meetings, to try to raise the $30,000 needed to pay all the expenses. She did, and God met the need. And then guess what happened.

The last night of the meetings there was a bomb threat where the military police made everyone leave the building and they brought in the bomb squad looking for bombs.

By God's grace nothing happened, the expenses had been met, and the meetings ended up outside with everyone singing and worshipping God.

After this I was asked to minister at the base chapel. I was so prayed up from praying so much, that when I ministered, the Spirit of God just flowed from me to meet the needs of the people. The gifts of the Spirit were flowing through me. I experienced the Holy Spirit physically on my body, exuding from within. It was an amazing experience. It felt awesome. When I finished ministering, to my amazement the people stood up and applauded, because God and his Spirit was manifesting very strongly that night.

When I returned to France, I began to be bored. There weren't many opportunities to minister, so I began to pray about what to do. In my heart, I felt I should do some healing meetings, but I was afraid to step out in faith and just start doing healing meetings. So then, God put in my heart that we could start passing out thousands of tracts to people.

I earnestly began praying for God to provide the money to buy tracts. Nothing happened. As I was praying, the Lord spoke and said, "I don't see any faith". I immediately knew the Lord wanted me to show actions of faith so that he could work to provide the tracts.

Since I now needed thousands of tracts, I asked Dorothy McClay, a graduate of Christ for the Nations Bible Institute, where I could purchase some good Christian tracts for witnessing. She told me the name of a Christian bookstore in Paris.

We then decided to go to the Christian bookstore. I didn't have any money, only my metro subway ticket. When we arrived at the bookstore, they only had a few samples, so I ordered several thousand tracts. You didn't have to pay for the tracts until they came in. They would come from Belgium, so this would give the Lord some time, and me time, to bring in the money or get the money to pay for the tracts. They said they would call the house when the tracts came in.

A few days later the bookstore called and said the tracts were in. I said I would pick them up in a few days. I then seriously began to pray. I still didn't have any money to pay for the tracts. Three days later the bookstore called and said they needed me to come and pick up the tracts. I said, "I will be there today", and hung up the phone.

As I was wondering why I said I would be there today, the doorbell rang. A postman had a package for me. I took the package. Inside the package was $100 that my father sent for my Christmas present. So, I immediately went and picked up the tracts that day, just as I had said. Another new experience of speaking faith and it happening the same day.

Scott Barton, Janis Bonds, (Celia's daughter) and I then passed out lots and lots of tracts to people in Rambuillet, France, and in Paris, France.

One day I wanted to see what would happen to one tract, so I left one tract on a seat in the metro subway station. I wanted to see what effect one track could have.

I saw seven people pick up the tract, read it and put it down before someone took it with them. I rejoiced when I saw this, for I knew that God was really using these tracts to plant seeds in these people of France.

Months later, when I felt it was time to return to the USA, I needed to purchase a plane ticket from Paris, France, back to Dallas, Texas. I began looking for the cheapest flight possible.

The normal airfare one way was over $800, which I didn't have. But God was faithful. I discovered a charter company that had a couple of empty seats to fly from Paris to New York City. All I had to pay was $160.

I really felt great that the Lord had provided such a cheap flight.

When I went to the airport I had to wait an extra six hours, but I was happy because the price was so cheap. I then discovered a lot of these people had paid $1200 - $1600 for a round trip to Paris. Some had been waiting for over 20 hours, because they kept delaying the plane's takeoff.

We finally boarded the plane and I thought we would see a movie or something. I was surprised - - not only was there no movie, but one hour after departure the stewardess served everyone some peanuts and soft drinks. Then for the rest of the nine-hour flight, there was nothing to eat or drink.

I was still rejoicing because it was such a cheap flight. Then there was an electrical short in the kitchen, so they could not heat anything in the kitchen. After that, the water on the plane froze, so that no one could even get a glass of water or flush the toilet. I was sitting at the front of the plane and the floor was so cold I had to lift my feet off the floor.

The situation began to get so bad, that several people began to make jokes and start having fun, they were afraid people would start to panic. The result from all the chaos and potentially life-threatening circumstances was one of the most fun flights I have ever had in my life. This was another experience of God taking something bad and making it good and exciting for me. I loved it.

My only regret from this flight was not contacting the FAA in Washington D.C. about this company. About two years later, lots of American military personnel were being carried by the same charter airline company; the plane crashed, killing all on board. I believe it had to be because of poor maintenance.

When I arrived in New York City, I had to go through U. S. Customs. I was traveling alone and obviously an American, with a Texas accent, so when the customs officer asked me if I was a spy, I thought he was joking with me, so I said," "yeah, sure I am".

I soon discovered he wasn't joking. I was detained for what seemed like hours, but I am sure it was less than thirty minutes. He went through every bit of luggage, every book, every little thing I had, he examined. He then gave me a serious lecture about not joking with the customs officers. A lesson I learned quickly and never repeated. I was so scared... but God.

I have never been so glad to leave the customs area, as I was that day. Because of all the delays, the plane I had planned to take had already departed, but by the Grace of God, I had not purchased my ticket for this final leg of the trip.

I would then have to wait another 12 hours in the New York airport to take the 10 AM plane to Dallas. But this delay turned out to be a real blessing. I met a young French lady who wasn't a Christian and had to spend the night in the airport as well. So, this French lady who didn't know Christ, felt that she could trust me. For the next 8 or 9 hours, we talked and kept each other company. I could share Christ with a French person, even in the U. S. I knew the Lord wanted to reach the French for the Lord. The young lady didn't pray to receive Christ, but I knew I could plant the seed, and believed that it would later be harvested by her receiving Christ.

God is so wonderful. After I had shared Christ with her, we decided we should go toward the airline counters to check our baggage. I knew I could fly to Dallas on one airline that left at 10 O'clock, but I really wanted to leave on the seven O'clock flight on another airline.

The French lady knew the situation with my finances because neither of us had much money, so I told her "well, I am going to see what happens". I knew I didn't have enough money for the flight at 7 AM, but the Lord may do something. I went to the counter of the airlines and casually told him the situation. He asked me how much I had, and I said $76.00. He said okay, that's fine.

So, I then had a greatly discounted airfare to Dallas. I said my goodbyes to the French lady and boarded the plane to Dallas. She had a witness to God's grace and favor in helping me get a ticket at half price.

The Grace of God was on me to witness, for on the next two connecting flights to Dallas I would really give an effective witness to two other people.

That night was a Sunday night. I really wanted to go to church, yet I had not slept for about 70 hours. After church, I returned home and went to sleep; I had not slept in over 72 hours. I was not tired because I was not going in my strength. I was going in the strength of the Lord.

As I was going to church that night with my mother, I realized that I was experiencing another miracle. For me to not sleep in 72 hours was a real miracle of the Lord. I knew I could not do it in my own strength. It was just another little miracle that the Lord did, so he could accomplish his will.

Another notable miracle, that I thought was great, took place in Paris. It happened with me and my interpreter, Jean Luc. After one service was over, I was singing in tongues or singing in the Spirit.

Suddenly Jean Luc looked surprised, and said Kyle, you were singing in French.

I said I was? I was just singing in the Spirit, but I didn't realize I was singing in French. I didn't really speak French. I had taken French in high school, but I could understand a limited amount in French. This only happened one time, but I thought it was great. I was singing in tongues and sang in French.

Another miracle of grace, that I learned and experienced in Paris, was the grace to not commit sexual sin. At the time, I was unmarried and in my twenties. Well, to be perfectly honest, there was much temptation in France. The subway advertisements had a lot of nudity and even family-oriented photography businesses had pictures of bare breasted women hanging in their windows. The French are very casual about sex and the display of the human body. This of course, begins to work on anyone after a time.

One day as I was praying. The Lord spoke to me and said, "you are in lust". I said "Lord, I am not". The Lord said nothing further. That day the Lord opened my eyes and really showed me that I really was in lust.

I then began to pray about what to do, to stop the desires I had of seeing all this nudity. The Lord spoke to me something which has helped me all my life. He said if you don't like chocolate, you won't be tempted with chocolate. This was a phrase I heard Bill Kaiser, one of my Bible school teachers, talk about in Bible College quite often. At first, I thought Lord, you must be crazy.

I then saw what the Lord was talking about. If I didn't want to see the nudity, I would not be tempted. So, I began to say to myself, "I don't like to see these things".

I would hear a little voice say, "you are lying, you know you like to see these things". I would say "no, the new man, the new creature in Christ Jesus doesn't like to see these things. I have new desires. I do not desire to see these things". After I said this, a few thousand times, in a few days, I began not to want to see these things.

I had victory over the lust in about three days. This

simple principle has literally saved me from sin many times in different countries, as well as in the U.S.

Also, along these lines, I was praying about not wanting to fall into the sex sin that other people had fallen into, when the Lord spoke something so very clear. I know it saved me from many sex sins. The Lord said you will never do something unless you first think about it. Just don't think about doing it, and you won't do it.

These two principles the Lord gave me, probably saved my ministry many times. I have even had a "Christian" woman want to rape me one time. I have had prostitutes grab my private parts as I witnessed in the streets. I have even had a prostitute come into my motel room with her own key in the middle of the night, while I was in bed with just my underwear on. It was in part because of these two principles, but in the times, I would be weak, God sovereignly protected me from falling into a sex sin, by his power and grace.

One time it was hilarious. It was just the grace and mercy of God. The lady who is now my wife was visiting me in the U.S.A. from Chile. We both loved each other and felt passionately about each other. Well, one night I had already decided that we would have sex. I think perhaps she had also contemplated that we would have sex before she returned to Chile, as well. What happened was totally the grace of God.

That night, the last night before she left, we were going to go for a walk in the country, beside a little private lake, which is where I was building a house for us. Every night we would go for a walk or do something to be alone.

Well, each night we would use a mosquito repellent to keep the mosquitoes away. That night we put on the mosquito repellent, the same as any other night, but this night, every time I would kiss her for more than one second, I would start coughing. I tried to kiss her for several seconds and coughed so much I was almost sick. The entire night we could not even kiss. We were both so frustrated.

God knew our weaknesses and gave me a supernatural allergy that only lasted one night. The Lord knows how to deliver the Godly from temptation. This was just a sovereign work of God's grace. I had prayed God would keep me from temptation and sin, and he did what I prayed. It wasn't me, but it was God's grace that was working in me. I was experiencing God's grace.

CHAPTER IX

MY NAZARETH

The town of Nazareth was where Jesus grew up. This is the town where Jesus could do little in ministry. In the Nazareth of Jesus, they wanted to kill him at one time. I had my Nazareth as well. My Nazareth was Terrell, Texas, USA.

After I committed my life to Christ, no one tried to kill me in Terrell, therefore I had far greater acceptance than Jesus had in his Nazareth. But because it was my hometown, I felt I was not able to fulfill what the Lord wanted to do there. Yet a person's home town can be one of the greatest schools of education that prepare you for dealing with rejection and lack of acceptance. If I had not experienced the rejection of my Nazareth, I probably would not have had enough character to accomplish what I was later to accomplish. I want to share some of the memorable experiences and miracles of my Nazareth.

I pastored a church in Terrell a couple of times. I never had great success there, but I learned a lot and saw some interesting, and sometimes, funny things happen.

We had a large building; it was three and one-half stories in the downtown section of Terrell. Terrell was a small town of about 10 - 15,000 people. The church was small with only a handful of people. I did a little bit of everything to cause the church to grow, but almost nothing worked.

One Saturday night I was at a Full Gospel Business Men's meeting. The man teaching and sharing his testimony made a statement about Jesus praying all night long. After he said this, it just stayed with me, so I decided for the first time in my life to go to the church and pray all night long. After about 3 hours, I had prayed just about everything and every way I knew to pray. I was now praying a lot in the Spirit and trying to stay awake.

In my attempt to stay awake and keep praying, I decided to go to pray on the flat roof of the church. It was about four stories tall, so it was a great place to look out over the city and pray.

It was about four o'clock in the morning, I was praying in the Spirit, sitting down at the front part of the building. I could see U.S. 80, the four-lane highway down below. While I am praying, there is absolutely no traffic on the street, four stories below.

Then a car came down the street. A man got out of the car right in front of the church. He was obviously drunk and began to relieve himself right in front of the church in the middle of the street. At first, I was shocked at his using the bathroom, in the middle of a four-lane highway, but there was no one around, except me. He obviously couldn't see me. As I sat wondering what to do, an idea came into my mind, which I quickly acted on.

I began to shout with an authoritative voice "repent and be saved in the name of Jesus". During the man relieving himself, he hears a voice coming from on high. He looks up, and seeing no one, gets in his car and leaves.

Every time I think about this I laugh. I am sure the man

thought he had heard an audible voice from God. I am sure he repented and committed his life to Christ, because of a funny sense of humor that our God gave me. The Lord is sometimes hilarious.

The next morning, I was amazed. The church had more people than it had ever had. The Lord was trying to teach me the importance of prayer.

In the same church building, a few months later, I was praying in my office. The office overlooked the sanctuary down below. I was to preach that Sunday night, so I was praying after I had prepared my message.

I was fervently praying in the spirit. As I looked out the windows of my office into the sanctuary, I saw a beautiful white angel about 15 feet tall. The angel was dressed in white and had two wings. It is difficult to describe the wings, other than to say they were like bird's wings, but on the underside of the wings, I could see the muscles of the angel, which controlled the wings. The muscles were covered with a very fine fur about one-half inch thick. The fur, the wings, and the garment were all white.

When I saw this awesome creature of God, the awe and the fear of God came on me so great that I was literally breathless and drew back. I think the angel probably wanted to give a message to me, but I was so shocked and surprised at seeing the awesome creature of God, that I only saw this angel for a moment of time.

I couldn't understand why the church wasn't growing. I was experiencing the supernatural and had even seen an angel in the church. Yet, the people stayed away in droves. After pastoring nine months, the Lord spoke to me to leave the church.

I was stubborn and determined to make this work, so I said "Lord, you must confirm this to me in the Sunday morning service in some way". As I was preaching the message, we began to hear a sound from above. Then suddenly, electrical lights burst, and fire fell from the ceiling.

I saw fire literally fall on one lady's head. After cutting off the electricity and making sure the fire was out, I told the people and repented because of being in unbelief about what God had spoken.

I now had seen and experienced fire falling from above as a sign from God. It wasn't anything like I had expected. It was a natural thing, yet supernatural. After this experience, we joked about it, saying we had actually seen fire fall from above in the church. We had fires, but not the revival fires of the Holy Spirit that we wanted.

Several years later, after I had been to France, Jamaica, and Mexico, I felt the Lord wanted me to start a church in Terrell. This time when I started to pastor I was wiser, more experienced, and had graduated from Bible College. I thought this time they will surely accept my ministry in my hometown, or my Nazareth. I really wanted to see my hometown receive Christ and have genuine revival. This time I was far more professional and knew how to do more things. We mailed out hundreds and hundreds of tracts to people. We purchased a computerized telephone machine to call everyone in the city, many times. We advertised in the newspaper. We had healing services. We had guest speakers. We had all night prayer meetings. We had concerts. We supported missions.

In less than a year after the church was started we had about 50 people, once it was up to about 70.

Then the Lord spoke to me to leave in February to go to Chile. So, I left this church and another person became Pastor, when I went to Chile. Then the Lord spoke to me to do some things in Africa, so I figured I needed to leave the church board. I had stopped pastoring a couple of years earlier, but

I was still on the board making decisions. When I finally left the church, resigning my position as an elder in the church, the church closed within two months.

I had learned that success is not success without a successor. The church needed a different person to be Pastor after I left. Apparently when I resigned from the board the Lord no longer would continue supporting the church. This made me curious, but my mind was now on Africa and South America.

I had to learn that if people don't receive you or your ministry, you cannot force it to happen. You can be called, anointed of God, see the supernatural, teach and preach the word, be evangelistic, and yet not see success.

Nothing will happen if people don't respect you. The people of Nazareth did not respect Jesus. They said this is Mary's son, we know his brothers. Jesus is just a carpenter, he is nobody special. What pride this Jesus has, thinking he is something when he is nothing. They said of me - this is Teddy's son. This is Jimmy's son. This is Thelma's grandson. This is Era's grandson. We know his brothers Kirk and Keith. We know his cousins and his uncles. Kyle is just a carpenter. What pride he must have, thinking he is something, when he is nothing. They didn't understand they should respect the position of ministry, even if they don't respect the person.

I had to learn to love people and forgive people when they hurt me, when they lied about me, when they had no respect for me or the office God had called me to.

I had to learn to deal with rejection before God would be able to exalt the ministry. My Nazareth was probably the greatest school of life, I could ever experience. I longed to see real revival come to Terrell, but apparently, God would have to send someone else to accomplish this task.

CHAPTER X

THE JAMAICA JOURNEYS

Many times, we don't understand what the Lord really wants us to do. We only understand a part of it. This was the case with Jamaica. If one person prayed to receive Christ during my ministry, my ministry would not have been a failure. The Lord once said, "when you learn the value of one soul, I can trust you with millions". Part of my Jamaica experience was to help me learn the value of one soul.

The first trip to Jamaica came about in a very unusual way. I believe it was in May of 1984, a young lady introduced herself to me at church. We both were going to the same church in Dallas at the time. She said she was praying and saw me in a vision. We talked a little while and later she came to a Bible study I was having at my home. After the lesson, we were all talking about different things. She asked me if she could talk to me privately. I said yes, of course. She then explained that she had seen me in a vision and was shown that we were to get married.

The problem she had with the vision, was that she was engaged to someone else, when she had the vision and still was.

I said I would pray about it. We met a couple of times, and once talked in her car until about 7 AM. We had a good relationship with each other, but I thought it was just good Christian fellowship. I liked her, but I really didn't quite believe it, and I don't think she really did either.

So out of a desire to give God the opportunity to confirm the word, or this vision to me, I happened to see a contest for a trip for 2 to Jamaica. I said "Lord, if you really want us to get married, as she had seen in her vision, cause me to win this trip to Jamaica". After all, we would need to go somewhere for a honeymoon. I then entered the contest.

On the 4th of July weekend, I received a phone call. I had won the trip to Jamaica. I was to go the first week of August. The hotel, airfare, transfers, taxis, etc. would all be paid by the travel agency. I was shocked, surprised, happy and scared.

Only I knew what I had prayed and said to the Lord. Everyone thought it was great that I had won the trip, but until now, no one ever heard the story of why I won the trip.

I was afraid to get married, and I barely knew the girl. She was engaged and was going to Rhema Bible Training Center that fall. I didn't want to create any problems; after all, this might be just a coincidence. This might not have really been a confirmation of the vision she had.

Out of my guilt, because I really felt in my heart that the vision was right, and the vision was of the Lord, I planned a 2-person witnessing trip instead. I really did not want to get married, I did, but I didn't. I never again talked to her after I won the trip. That summer she moved, and I had no address or telephone numbers. My self-confidence was so low that I could not trust it to be from the Lord, even though I felt good about it in my spirit.

I let my fear rule me, instead of being led by the Spirit. But God is ever merciful. So, I felt I must redeem the trip and use it to win people to Christ.

Since I was in disobedience and won a trip to Jamaica, from the Lord for a honeymoon, but wasn't going on a honeymoon, I felt I couldn't go for a vacation, but must redeem it in some way. So, I asked Troy Schooley, one of the boldest witnesses for the Lord that I knew, to go with me.

Sometimes when Troy and I were together, he would motion people to lower their windows, in their car, when we would be stopped at a signal light. They would open their window and he would share Christ with them.

The day before I was to go to Jamaica, I was going home from work. I was on staff at the church in Farmers Branch. As I was driving down the freeway, thinking about witnessing in Jamaica, I turned to take another freeway and had to go on the highest ramp, where two large interstate highways intersect. A lot of times, older people would drive very slowly over this ramp, because it was so high.

As I approached this ramp, there was a car about four vehicles ahead of me, going very slowly. As it went toward the top of the ramp I thought it was probably some older person afraid of this ramp. It was a very high bridge probably over 100 feet high.

Then suddenly the car stopped. A young man about 30 years old got out of the car and dove head-first off the highest point of the bridge. He plunged to his death as the cars of two highways below saw him come crashing down to his death; a suicide.

This would be the first of several suicides that I would come in close contact with. Another happened in Santiago, Chile, when Denny Martinez and I were going to arrange my marriage to Veronica in Santiago with some government officials. Another happened by a friend of mine that committed suicide after several months of marriage.

These people literally threw their life away. What a waste. What a shame. They didn't understand the value or the purpose of life. They could not have understood their value here on earth, or their purpose or reason for living here on earth.

I was once in Corpus Christi, Texas, going to visit some friends of mine, Peggy and Tom Christian. As I walked on the sidewalk in front of their apartment, I saw a young girl crying. She said, "I want to kill myself". I led her to Peggy and Tom's apartment where Peggy and I tried to console her, comfort her and lead her to Christ. She began to tell us her story.

She was 18 years of age. She had already been married twice. Her second marriage was to a sailor who she hadn't seen in several months. He also, apparently, had abandoned her. From the time, she could remember, her father would force her to have sex with him. He even gave her to his friends to have sex with her. She also had been raped a couple of other times in her young life. She wanted to kill herself, for she had no reason to live.

I sat amazed as I heard her story yet believing and knowing in my heart it was true. I prayed in my heart, saying Lord, what can I say? I said, if I were you, I am sure I would also want to commit suicide. If anyone has reason to commit suicide, you do.

The only thing I can say is that you were not born by accident. The Lord has a plan and purpose for your life. God created you for a purpose here in the earth. There is a reason for you to live. As I said these words, I could see hope enter her eyes and her eyes light up. She had prayed to accept Christ, but she had never been told that the Lord had a plan and a purpose for her life.

Well, let's get back to Jamaica. Troy and I arrived, ready to witness, yet we had almost no success. I now understand that you must witness because of being led by the Lord, not out of guilt, to be effective. We witnessed to many people, yet almost nothing happened.

Finally, as I was walking alone to one tent meeting held by an Assembly of God Church, a prostitute came up to me. I shared Christ with her and she prayed to receive Christ. I then prayed with her to receive the baptism of the Holy Spirit, to give her the power to live for the Lord. I left her that night as she was speaking in tongues. Praise God!

Before our return to the U. S., Troy sincerely talked about returning to Jamaica as a missionary. I now felt the trip was worthwhile, for one person had prayed to receive Christ.

Several years later, the Lord would send me to Jamaica again. But this time I was sent. The first time I was in Montego Bay and Ocho Rios, so this time I decided to fly in to Kingston, Jamaica.

My father, James Leatherwood took me to the airport and we prayed over my bags before I left.

Well, things were going fine from Dallas to Miami. At Miami I had a few problems regarding my ticket, but nothing major. As I boarded the plane for Kingston, Jamaica, I felt that I had stepped out of God's perfect will, so I started praying. The plane was taxiing for takeoff when it suddenly stopped in the middle of the airport.

As I looked out my window, I see an airport vehicle with my baggage on it. They had stopped the plane, so they could bring my bags and another person's bags onto the plane.

I rejoiced, for I knew God was with me. But I still felt out of God's perfect will. When the plane arrived in Kingston, I was absolutely convinced I was in the wrong place.

There have only been two places in the world when I arrived that I felt I had to leave and leave quickly. One was Kingston, Jamaica. The other place was Panama City, Panama.

At the airport, I knew this was not where God wanted me. I had such a strange sense of fear, almost an impending doom, if I stayed in Kingston.

Immediately I went to a cheap hotel. I began to fast and pray. I knew I was out of God's perfect will. So, I prayed and stayed; until I knew where the Lord wanted me to go.

The Lord spoke to me and said, "go to Christ for the Nations". I knew this was at Montego Bay, so I immediately arranged to go to Montego Bay.

The trip to Montego Bay was relatively uneventful but it had the potential to be disastrous, if I had defended myself or even white people in general. One person on the bus tried to provoke me to anger the entire six-hour trip. I knew he wanted to get into a fight with me because I was white. But God did not allow it to happen. I knew several black men on the bus would have loved to help this man try to beat up this lone white man, me. After all I was the only white man on this small bus of about 15 people, so they were talking all kinds of trash that would make any white man upset. But God was faithful.

I tried to concentrate on the beauty of Jamaica. Jamaica is a very pretty country.

After spending a night at a hotel in Montego Bay, Jamaica, I made my way to Christ for the Nations. I knew about this school because I would visit some of the meetings they had at their large school in Dallas. I had no idea what the Lord wanted with CFNI, but I was willing. So, I talked with several people on staff and filled out an application.

I then learned I would have to pay about $400 a month and work forty hours a week for them and get paid nothing, in return for the privilege to stay there.

The secretary then told me about a hotel, the Hotel Caribe, at Reading. She said she would call for me. After negotiations with the manager, I could stay at this nice hotel for $375 per month. Some people were paying up to $150 per night. So, this was really a blessing! This was less than CFNI and I could spend all my time writing or praying or doing whatever the Lord wanted me to do.

The Lord had really blessed me by giving me a room at this hotel. It was air conditioned, had a private beach, a jetty into the water, and a swimming pool. All of this for less than CFNI required, and I didn't have to work 40 hours a week for them.

I did volunteer and help CFNI some with some construction work, but I had been fasting for about 2 weeks and almost passed out because of the heat. It had been years since I had done such physical work, so I felt that the Lord had sent me to CFNI, just so I could find this hotel.

The Lord caused many people to receive Christ at this hotel. As I was working on a book and doing a lot of fasting, the Lord began to open doors of relationship with people.

One day a friend of mine, from Christ for the Nations, and I were sitting by the swimming pool of this hotel. We were just talking and fellowshipping, when a young man from Canada came up. The man from Canada, I will call Mark. He was talking about how stressed out he was and had not slept in about a week.

My friend took the religious witness approach and said, "You need Jesus, the Prince of Peace". Mark immediately rejected this as the answer to his stress. My friend left and then the Lord began to create a relationship between Mark and myself.

For the next 8 hours, Mark and I talked. We found many common points of agreement in our lives. I shared some of the things in my life, not as counsel, but as a friend talking to his friend. Mark had even thought about suicide, his wife wanted to leave him. He had many problems. That night we parted as new friends. He said he would do what we talked about.

The next morning, I was down at the pool drinking my Coke, sharing Christ with another couple that had become recent friends. Mark shouted across the pool - "Kyle - I did what you said last night, I feel like I have been born again or something". I then went over to talk with him further. Mark was there about a week. When he left, he said he was going back to Canada to preach.

The other couple I was sitting with is also an interesting story. They came to the hotel after staying at a private guesthouse. I will call them Dick and Jane. They told me about the following experience they had. They left the guesthouse they had been staying at because of many types of demon manifestations and the owner of the guesthouse apparently became possessed and attacked them, trying to kill them. They had never believed in demon spirits until they came to Jamaica. They were relieved that they met someone who knew some things about these evil spirits.

As we were eating dinner at the hotel restaurant later that evening, I began sharing how I prayed to receive Christ. I shared how I had prayed years earlier the sinner's prayer saying "Jesus, I ask you to forgive me of my sin and come into my heart". I then said, it felt like a thousand pounds of weight was lifted off my shoulders.

Jane suddenly reached across the table, grabbed my arm and said, "tell me that prayer, tell me that prayer, I want to pray that prayer". She was born and raised in the USA and had never heard of the simple prayer to receive Christ. I felt that she and her "husband" needed to pray to receive Christ without anyone around, but only the Lord and them. The next day she said they had prayed and had felt such a difference that it was amazing.

Another problem with Jane, was apparently a demon spirit would manifest through her, after the experience at the guest house. I instructed her about the power of Jesus and that Jesus wanted her to be free from the devil and his power. I told her about resisting the devil and she needed to resist him and not be afraid.

Previously for several nights in a row, she would start acting like a dog, urinating like a dog and even urinated about a gallon of urine at one time, which was naturally impossible. She was scared to death. After that night, she never had another problem. When she left, she was so glad she had come to the hotel, we had met, she received Christ, and was delivered from devils.

I didn't tell them because I wanted their faith in Christ, not me, but I prayed in tongues and fought the devil for several hours that night. I wanted her to believe that she, as a new Christian, had the power to resist the devil and he would flee from her. So, she resisted, and the devil fled. What part I had, God only knows.

Another night, as I walked out to the jetty to pray, I met a security guard working for the hotel. We began to talk briefly, and he suddenly said, "how can I be saved, I want to be saved". I then instructed him, and he prayed to receive Christ.

Once when I was in a taxi going to CFNI, I was witnessing and had the man at the point of praying to receive Christ, when he said, "I have prayed a similar prayer about seven times, but nothing has ever happened". I then explained that he had to pray from his heart, in faith. I told him if he really was serious about it, to get alone with God and pray with all his heart and that God would hear and he would be forgiven and be born again.

One day I decided to go down into Montego Bay and eat some shrimp at a restaurant. I had learned the best way to get people to leave you alone is to witness to them. A man came up, trying to sell drugs or get a prostitute for me. I began to witness, merely because I wanted him to leave me alone, but he was really interested in what I was saying. So, I began to tell of a lot of miracles I had seen in my life and what had happened to many other people when I prayed.

As I said this he said, "would you pray for a friend of mine?" I said yes. As I said yes, I saw a man in a wheelchair coming toward us, but a long way off. I thought, "I am so glad I don't have to pray for this man".

The wheelchair came closer as the man I was witnessing to say, "oh, here is my friend".

I tried to share Christ to the man in the wheelchair, but he didn't want to pray to receive Christ. I said, "Do you want me to pray for you to be healed"? He said, "Yes, you can". I tried to hear some faith but heard none. Reluctantly I began to pray for him and laid hands on him. I so wanted to hear some faith or expectancy of some kind, for I knew I really wasn't in faith.

I was full, I had just eaten a nice meal. I didn't feel spiritual at all. But as I prayed, I felt the power of God go into his body.

He had been stabbed in his back by a girlfriend and had not been able to move his legs for years. His legs were tied into the wheelchair. I then told him to pick up his legs and begin to move them, which he did. God had restored his severed nerves. He could now move his legs. I then asked him if he wanted to pray and receive Christ, and he said no. I instructed him on some things, about what to do to strengthen his legs, before he tried to walk. Weeks later I saw him walking in Montego Bay.

Well, the Lord used me with other people in Jamaica as well. I also shared at a couple of churches and the Lord used me some other ways. The time came for me to leave and return to the U.S.

I would pay my hotel bill every month. It would include my cokes and some meals at the hotel. I knew I didn't have enough money to pay the bill, as I was preparing to leave. I went to the hotel desk and told them to prepare my bill. They started figuring my total on the bill, when a man came up and said, "This is for you".

It was an envelope that a friend had sent to me. I opened it up and found some money in it. I put the money in my pocket. Then the hotel clerk then said, "Here is your bill".

I took the money out and paid the bill. I had a little cash left over to pay for the taxi to the airport. When I arrived at the airport I had one dollar left over, which I used to buy a Coke at the layover in Miami.

At the airport in Jamaica I met a nice black lady in a wheelchair. You could tell she loved the Lord. She said she was there feeding the poor. She said she always had her purse open and never ran out of money as she fed the poor.

She said, "I know an angel comes and actually at times puts money in my purse". She went on to say,, "I never run out of money, as long as I feed the poor and keep my purse open". Then she stated, "if I close my purse, the angel can't put the money in my purse, so I always leave my purse open".

We continued talking and then she said she needed to leave. Another man came up and began to push her wheelchair to go to her plane. She went through an emergency door with direct access to the airport tarmac. As they shut the door I looked through the windows and they were nowhere to be found. I could not see this sweet lady anywhere, when she went through the door, she literally disappeared. I knew it must have been an angel.

As I write this story, I am sure God sent his angel to show me that I needed to always be feeding the poor, so the angels could come and bring money to me.

CHAPTER XI

FOCUS ON THE FAMILY

Many times, people are being "led by the Lord" and do many great things, but they never see God work in their family. God always has seasons or times of focus. At times the Lord has had me focus on my family. Let me share how the Lord has used me in some degree with my family.

In 1977 the Lord had been dealing with my mother for several months for her to return to Christ, for she was backslidden.

Someone had given her a little book called "The Game of Life and How to Play it", so she gave it to me. This was the book that caused me to pray to receive Christ. When I prayed for the Lord to forgive me of my sins and come into my heart, it felt as if a thousand pounds had been lifted off me.

Well, I shared this experience with Mother. My mother told me later, that this experience I had shared, motivated her to commit her life afresh to the Lord.

Months later, I would also receive the Baptism of the Holy Spirit and begin to speak in tongues. As I shared this experience with her, she began to sincerely cry out to the Lord for this same experience. The Lord, of course, heard her cry and she also received the Baptism of the Holy Spirit and began to speak in tongues.

The Lord used me many times regarding my mother. In part, because of my encouragement, she went to Bible College and even pastored a church.

In 1979, I was praying one day, and the Lord spoke to me through a scripture regarding "making yourself known to your own flesh", which I knew applied to my father. We saw each other about 3 or 4 times a year. You couldn't really call this knowing one another. The Lord put on my heart that I should visit my father and stepmother every week. So, for the next 10 months I would go to my father's house almost every Thursday night and have dinner with them. During the first few weeks I shared some things about the Lord.

I felt that my stepmother, Maxine, was about ready to receive Christ, but I knew my father wasn't ready. I felt that I could have led Maxine to a place of commitment to the Lord, but that this would have repelled my father from the Lord, for he wasn't ready yet. So, I knew I must wait until he was ready.

One night, as I was talking about Jesus' return, the end times and Bible prophecy about it, my father became upset and said, "I don't want to hear another thing in this house about the Lord".

So, I said nothing about the Lord for about 9 months. Yet, almost every Thursday I would go have dinner with them.

Finally, about 9 months later I sat down to eat with them and my father said, "do you want to say the blessing over the food"?

I said yes. I then said the blessing.

Around this time my father heard Kenneth Hagin talk about his experience of dying twice. The first time, when he was sick and died, he heard a voice apparently from an angel as he was being taken to Hell. It said, "Now is not your time".

He then returned to his body. He was still sick, but alive. Being raised in a church he thought he was saved.

At 17 years of age Kenneth Hagin didn't realize you had to be born again, to go to heaven. He thought you went to heaven because you were good. But Brother Hagin learned from his death experience that he could only go to heaven by being born again and placing his faith in Christ. This is exactly what my father needed.

My father was one of the most honest and good people you could ever meet, yet he discovered he would go to hell, not because he was bad, but because he had never received Christ and been born again.

After Kenneth Hagin prayed to receive Christ and to be born again, he died again.

This time he was being taken to Heaven, when again he heard a voice saying now is not the time. He then went back into his body and was alive.

Years later Maxine, my step mother, was talking to my mother, Teddy Hunt, and said that they were impressed with the joy of the Lord in me and that God used me to help bring them to Christ. She knew many things were going on that were bad, yet despite it all, I would have the joy continuously week after week.

One night I was visiting my grandparents' house when I felt I must ask my grandfather if he had ever prayed to receive Christ. He said no. He had been to church many, many times, but had never prayed to receive Christ. I asked him if he would pray with me for him to receive Christ, and he said yes. So, I led him in a prayer to receive Christ.

Another interesting story happened with my step mother's

son, Tim. We would only occasionally see each other, but I had prayed for him to be saved. So, one night I had a dream. In this dream, Tim was in church and had received Christ. A few days later I saw Tim and told him the dream. He wasn't too impressed with the dream, but I told him it was just a matter of time before he accepted Christ. I told him it would happen, I had no doubt about it.

Well, months later, Tim was working at a factory when suddenly the Holy Spirit physically came upon him. He committed his life to Christ and began to speak in tongues. I know my father and stepmother witnessed to him many, many times, but only God knows what each person needs to receive Christ.

Many of us planted seeds, but you can only truly be born again because the Holy Spirit is drawing you to Christ. At the time, Tim was ready, the Holy Spirit came upon him and he was born again.

I also had a part in four other people in my family praying to receive Christ. But because they stopped going to church and fell away from the things of the Lord, I prefer not to tell their stories.

Your family needs to see a difference in your life. If they see the difference, you can be effective. If you live like the devil, they sure won't listen to you.

One time another member of my family on my father's side came to me. She said, "we have all seen such a change in you, what really caused it?"

I then shared the simple story of how I prayed to receive Christ and was born again. She couldn't believe it was so simple. She didn't pray with me to receive Christ then, but I believe she did later.

The Lord has used me to lead more people to the Lord by accident, than most people do intentionally. I really can't take much credit, for sometimes I didn't even realize what was happening.

In 1984 I was invited to a wedding of a friend of mine. We had worked together at a church, so I thought he was a Christian.

When he introduced me to some people, he said I was the reason he had accepted Christ. I thought he was saved, but I had shared my testimony one day and the Holy Spirit used it to cause him to be born again. I was just talking about the Lord, and that resulted in him praying to receive Christ.

Sometimes there is nothing that you can do or can say, that will impact a person to receive Christ. I will never forget what happened to my half-brother, Keith's father, Leland. The man that taught us how to get away with crime.

My sister-in-law was in the hospital and we were all in the hospital room. I started sharing some about the Lord.

Leland began to say several things. He finally said, "there is no God, if there is a God, let him strike me dead now". Within a year, he had died. When people dare God to kill them, they are asking for problems, or death.

Many people in my family have seen Jesus. My great-grandmother, Vicie Purdue saw Jesus in her house before she died. My great aunt, Elva Cullins saw Jesus when she was sick and at the point of death at only 10 years of age. My mother, Teddy Hunt, saw Jesus one day, I believe as she was praising the Lord. My grandmother, Thelma Humphrey, had a dream where Jesus picked her up and had her in his arms. She had been sick ,and Jesus comforted her in a dream.

I heard T. L. Osborn preach;" When people see Jesus it will change their life".

So, I started praying that my half-brother, Keith would see Jesus. Within a couple of months of praying for this, it happened. His wife had been in the hospital. Keith was in the bed asleep. Keith awoke and saw Jesus standing in his bedroom.

Keith didn't commit his life to Christ after this, but he will never deny it. Several times when Keith would have some of his buddies around drinking beer, I would bring up the time that Keith saw Jesus. He would tell the story, and never deny the Lord. One day after I had talked to him, he threw his beer out of the truck and prayed and had an experience with God. But the pressures of those around him caused him to hide it.

Always remember that families should pray for each other.

As a teenager doing all sorts of bad things, I know my grandmothers, Era Leatherwood, and Thelma Humphrey were praying for me. I also know my Aunt Virginia was praying for me as well. You should always be praying for your family.

Many times, I would have dreams about people in my family dying, so I would begin to really pray for them. I know many times God has prolonged their lives because of the prayers of my family and me.

The Lord at times will place in our hearts to help our families in many ways. Let me tell of a couple of other miracles that God did as I tried to help my family.

I believe it was in 1979 my brother, Kirk, had just gotten married to Millie. They left Terrell, and about an hour down the road their car over-heated. Kirk called me, so I went and traded vehicles with him. I let him use my nearly new truck, while I took his older car back to Terrell to be repaired.

In a few weeks, we were going to meet each other in Jackson, Mississippi. He was coming from the Marine Base in North Carolina, and I was coming from Terrell. Jackson, Mississippi was about half way.

I left with a full tank of gas and about $20. I had loaned

Kirk my gas credit card, so I would get it when I picked up my truck. The car had just been repaired, so I didn't expect any problems. I was driving along the Interstate in the Louisiana Delta, when the unthinkable happened. The car started getting hot. The gauge went all the way over to HOT! HOT! HOT! I knew I only had enough money to buy gas. I didn't have enough money to pay for any kind of repair. I needed a miracle.

I was a young Christian and was at the point of panic. So, I cried out as loud as I could - JESUS, JESUS, JESUS. The third time I said Jesus, the presence of Jesus filled the car. I could feel and sense such a sweet love that I had never previously or afterward experienced. The love was so wonderful, so sweet, so compassionate, and so merciful.

I felt the size of an ant in his presence, yet not as me being wrong or bad, but as the Lord Jesus being so infinitely grander in love and in size.

As I looked at the temperature gauge, the temperature fell back to normal. I rejoiced and rejoiced; not just because of the miracle of the car, but because of the presence of Jesus being so absolutely wonderful.

I experienced this miracle because I was helping my family.

Shortly after I committed my life to Christ, I found myself wanting to help my grandparents and my family more than I had ever done before.

One time the floor in one of the bedrooms of my grandmother Leatherwood's house fell in. It was terrible. No one volunteered to fix it, so I decided I would do it. Well, after I started repairing the floor, I then decided to repair cracks in the walls and ceiling. I then decided I should paint it. Well, after I finished these things, the Lord opened the door for me to make some good money with a construction job. Not only that, while I was doing the repairs, the Lord made it very clear that I should not marry a young lady I was dating.

Therefore, the Lord brought direction and eventually money, because I was helping my grandmother. She couldn't afford to pay for this to be done, so the Lord had to reward me in some way, and this was the way he chose.

Another time, my grandparents on the Humphrey's side of the family had a problem. The floor of the shower fell in. No one could take a shower. They had another bathroom, but my grandfather always took a shower before this. He had property, but he didn't have the money to get this repaired. Well, I decided to repair this. I spent several days trying to repair it. I even made a seat in the shower, so my grandfather could sit down and take a shower. As I was working on the shower, something I had been praying to receive, happened.

I had been praying for the Baptism of the Holy Spirit and had entered faith that I had received it. Well, as I was praising God, singing a song, working on the shower, I began singing in other tongues. I started rejoicing, for I finally had experienced this blessing. From that day that I spoke in tongues to this day, I have never said one cuss word. All of this happened, in part, because I was helping my family.

For me, these things are little miracles, little signs and wonders. Many times, people are looking for something spectacular and miss the supernatural that is happening around them.

Shortly after receiving the Baptism of the Holy Spirit and the gift of speaking in tongues, Dennis Bennett, an Episcopal priest had taught that praying in tongues was praying the perfect prayer. When you don't know how to pray, always pray in tongues.

Well, my grandfather had given my mother a house, but it needed to have plumbing, electrical, and basically to be totally renovated. My mother didn't have any money. My grandfather didn't have the money, so I did what I had been taught. I would go into the house and pray in tongues, hours at a time. Sometimes I would pray just 15 - 30 minutes. But every week I would be praying in this house about it being completed for months.

To make a long story short, the house was eventually finished without anyone having to borrow money to finish it. I did most of the work, but the Lord is the one who provided everything for it to be done. My mother had a house free of payments, with no rent to pay.

I had learned this principal, so when I was ready to build my house, I started with $10 in my pocket. I had been praying to buy a house when my grandmother gave me a piece of land to build a house. Well, I would go and pray over this land in tongues.

I then saw an ad in the newspaper, someone wanted to give away a two-story building. You had to disassemble it. I went and saw the building and signed a contract for it. I had $10 when I started dismantling the building. I never once ran out of material. I always had material to work on the house.

I built this house using three principles. The first was to pray about it in the spirit. The second was to put action with my faith. The third was to do what was possible. The impossible thing of building a house became possible as I did what was possible. I started building a 2700 square foot house, not counting porches or balconies with $10 in my pocket. I just kept doing what was possible.

Several years later I gave the house to the ministry, then sold the house and put the money into the radio station I started in Sierra Leone, West Africa.

When a family agrees, great miracles can happen. I will never forget what happened one time when my grandmother

Thelma, my mother Teddy and I prayed.

We lived in the country. My grandfather had some cows and horses, but when he was older he sold his cows and only had a couple of horses. The fences were bad because there wasn't the money to build new fences. Well, whenever the female horses or mares were in heat, the male horse of my grandfather, would try to find some way to get out of the pasture and get to these other mares. Sometimes it would take several people to trap the horse and rope him. We would then have to tie the rope to a vehicle and literally pull this horse back to the pasture. This would sometimes take hours to accomplish.

So, one day, my grandmother called the house and said the horses were out. She said she was coming down to the house because she needed some help to get the horses back in the pasture. Within a few minutes, she, my mother and I were together at the house.

We decided to pray and agree that the horses would get back into the pasture quickly and easily. We prayed, loosed the angels and commanded the horses to go back into the pasture. As we walked out the door I could seed these horses running back toward our pasture. I ran to the gate, opened the gate and the horses ran into the pasture. This was such a great miracle.

Few people could understand, outside our family, how great a miracle this was. This one horse would fight tremendously returning into the pasture. Many times, he would have blood around his neck because of him fighting the rope tied around his neck, that was necessary to lead him back to the pasture. Yet, this time God sent his angels and brought them into the pasture.

The Bible is clear that if any 2 or 3 agree in prayer as touching anything, that they would ask, it would happen. After all, this is what families are to be for to help one another.

CHAPTER XII

THE MIRACLE OF MARRIAGE

My wife is a very private person and was raised so that you don't talk about your personal life to other people. So, she would shoot me if I told many of the answers to prayer regarding our marriage. But let me tell you the story, of what God had to do, to get us married.

I was ministering at a church in Santiago, Chile, when I saw Veronica. I heard a little voice saying, "She will be your wife". I thought to myself, this is just me, but just in case it is God, I had better go talk to her after the service.

Not knowing this, before I went up to the platform to minister, Veronica saw my head from behind as I was sitting down. She heard also that he will be your husband. This was the first time she had visited the church and did not know I was going to be the speaker. She said Lord if this is really you, cause him to come to me right after the service. And I did.

So, our relationship started differently than most. Her English wasn't very good, and my Spanish wasn't very good. Yet, despite cultural problems, language problems, and her mother not wanting her to marry me, we would eventually get married, about 5 years later.

It was an on and off relationship. She would say yes that we would get married, and then because her mother was so against her marrying me, she would change her mind. This went on for several years. I finally said, forget it.

We were supposed to have been married in Dec 1991, when I went to Chile the second time. I had told my supporters and church we were to get married and she had said yes. A friend of hers, Graciella even had a dream in Chile, saying we were to get married in December, when I came there in 1991. Well Veronica's mother was dead set against her marrying me, so to make a long story short we did not get married.

This caused me to lose a lot of credibility in the ministry, after all, I had said this was the will of God, etc. etc. Some people had even given me money for the trip, because we were to get married. So, this decision not to get married, made by Veronica and her mother, cost me a lot of support for the ministry as well as quite an emotional toll.

In 1994 The Lord spoke to me again and told me to go back to Chile. I first went in 1989 but the focus was to be ministry, not marriage. This time he told me specifically to go and that I would get married when I went. I thought God would bring someone else into my life, not Veronica. As far as I was concerned, it was finished with her.

Well, I went back to Santiago as the Lord instructed me. I was staying with some friends of mine, Angelica and Mariano Arancibia. I first met them in 1989 and we had become good friends. Their family showed me more about love than I had seen anywhere.

After being in Santiago for a day, I decided to visit Pastor Rafael Martinez, a friend of mine. So, after our meeting I decided to return to where I was staying.

I was in the subway minding my own business, sitting in the metro train. Then the Lord spoke and said, "I really want you to get married to Veronica, as a sign to you that this is me, I want you to get off at the next Metro station and within five minutes, you will see Veronica." I decided to do what God said. I thought well this is easy to prove if this is from God or just me. The odds of her being here now would be astronomical. So, I left the train at the next stop. As I was going up the steps of the metro station, I looked and saw Veronica. We talked and went and had a Coke together. When we parted, Veronica asked me if she would see me again, and I said I didn't know.

A couple of weeks later I was praying. The Lord spoke and said, "you still don't know if it is really me telling you to marry Veronica". So, he reminded me about a park in Providencia. He said to go there at 5:30 PM order a Coke and that Veronica would come to me within 15 minutes. I went to the park. I sat down at a table and ordered a Coke. In about 10 minutes, I saw Veronica walking down the street. She walked straight to me. I then began to take it seriously. The same thing happened one more time, before Veronica and I started dating again.

After I told Veronica about these signs, she started to get me to commit, to getting married. I still needed something more.

So, one night I had a dream. In the middle of the dream, Jesus appeared in a vision and said ,"I have given you my life, I have given you my death, I have given you the clothes off my back, I have given you my all, why do you stall"? I knew I had been stalling, and Veronica had even asked me that day why I was stalling. After seeing Jesus in this dream, that became a vision, I repented for the next several hours. We then were married in a few weeks.

CHAPTER XIII

A SUPERNATURAL MINISTRY

Shortly after I prayed to receive Christ in 1977, reading the Bible changed my life. I was raised a Southern Baptist, so I was taught that the Bible is to be believed. Pastor Fineout made it clear that everyone should believe the Bible as the inspired word of God. If you had to choose between what men said and what the Bible said, you were to always, always believe the Bible. This teaching eventually ruined me for most Baptist churches, but it prepared me for a supernatural ministry.

I was reading my Bible one day in August 1977 when I read John 14: 12. Jesus said "He that believeth in me, the works that I do shall he do also, and greater works than these shall he do because I go unto the Father". As I read it, in context, Jesus was clearly talking about doing the miracles that he was doing. Jesus clearly stated that believers would do this. I knew I believed in Jesus, but I had never seen a miracle and didn't know anyone personally who ever talked about experiencing a miracle. I was in a dilemma. Either I was to believe the Bible and believe Jesus wanted me doing miracles, seeing miracles and experiencing miracles or my only other choice was to believe the Bible wasn't true.

My relationship with the Lord was so real that if the Bible weren't true, it wouldn't change my belief in the Lord Jesus. I had had an experience with Jesus, but how could I know if the Bible was true and in fact, the Word of God?

I began to pray after I read this verse many times, to see if it actually said what I thought it said. I then said, "Lord, either the Bible is true and I will do the works of Jesus, or the Bible isn't true". I said, "If the Bible isn't true, kill me now, because I have nothing to base my life on". I prayed this with all my heart.

I know it is bad psychology and theology to pray this way, but I meant it. If the Bible wasn't true, I wanted to die.

I knew I needed something to live my life by. I knew I needed something to give me the direction and be the roadmap for my life. If the Bible wasn't the book to do this I really preferred to die. That night something happened. There was nothing supernatural, that I saw or experienced, but I knew something had changed. I knew my life would never be the same. Within months, nearly everything I knew or believed about the supernatural would change.

I had truly believed what I was taught as a Baptist, and it eventually ruined me for most Baptist Churches. Four months later, I had received the Baptism of the Holy Spirit and spoke in tongues. Within 2 years I had received the call to ministry and was even pastoring a small church. It was then I experienced being anointed with the Power of God.

I was returning from a seminar at a church in Dallas, Texas. I had been fasting for several days. I felt the Lord wanted to do something different in my life. Bill Swadd, a millionaire businessman, as well as a pastor, had ministered that night and had laid hands on me. Yet, nothing seemed different.

My mother, Leon Pickens and I were praising God on the return hour long trip to Terrell. We were just singing and worshiping the Lord in the car, when my first anointing with power happened.

Suddenly I felt power, almost like electricity begin to enter my body. It felt as though several hundred thousand volts of power were surging through my body. I was sitting in the back seat of the car. I began to feel my body expand. My head began to touch the roof of the car. My knees began to hit the back of the front seat. The power was so intense that I literally began to grow to absorb the power of God, the anointing of power.

As the power continued flooding my body, I could barely breathe, my body was almost in pain, but not pain. I suddenly remembered a story about John Wesley. John Wesley was walking down the street in New York City, when suddenly the Power of God fell on him. He cried "Lord, stop", and the power stopped. I remembered when I read the story. I thought to myself I would never say stop to the power of the Lord. Everything in me wanted to cry out STOP LORD. I thought if I die, it will be a glorious death, but I will not say stop Lord. The power continued for minutes, but it seemed like hours.

Leon seemed a little skeptical. He could feel nothing while I was having such a powerful experience. As we arrived at his house to drop him off, my mother wanted me to stand beside Leon to see if I had actually grown, like I felt and was talking about. Leon was about 6'1", and I am normally 5' 9-1/2 to 5'10"". That night we were both the same height.

That night was a glorious night. Every time I moved my hands I could feel the tangible power, like electricity leave my hands. The taste of power, or electricity was in my mouth. It was a glorious experience of power that few have ever experienced. It was the anointing of power for the Bible says Jesus was anointed with the Holy Ghost and Power.

I would have fresh baptisms of power occasionally, but another unforgettable Baptism, or fresh anointing of power happened 15 years later when I was at a Rodney Howard-Browne meeting.

I had gotten so full of the Holy Spirit I was drunk, not with alcohol, I was intoxicated by the new wine. I had gotten drunk spiritually, many times during this series of meetings.

I had read about this experience happening to people in the Bible and throughout Christian history, wherever there was a great out pouring of the Holy Spirit. I had sung the old songs in the Pentecostal and Assembly of God churches that spoke of this, but I had never really experienced it for myself. I needed a refreshing and God gave it. I would get so drunk in the Holy Spirit, I could barely walk, and I would laugh and laugh. After this experience, some of those old songs came alive. This was in the summer of 1994.

I had become tired and weary because of the ministry, and this was a time of refreshing which I enjoyed and needed. But toward the end of this series of meetings, Rodney had laid hands on me and I ended up on the floor. I couldn't get up or move any part of my body. The presence and power of God was on me mightily. Then the intensity of power began to increase more and more. I felt as if I was enveloped in a Baptism of raw electricity or raw power. It was the same sense of unlimited unrestrained power I had felt 15 years earlier.

Again, the intensity of power was so great I wanted to cry out "stop". But I wouldn't and will never say no to God's power. As the power increased I could no longer feel any part of my body. My face was the only part that wasn't totally consumed by this power. I could have said stop or resisted it and it would have left. But I knew it was a fresh and more complete anointing of power. I was on the floor consumed by the power of God for about an hour. So many times, I wanted to say, "STOP LORD". But how could I say stop to God's fresh anointing of power.

Some people will surely say what difference did this anointing of power make. I can only say study the scriptures and you will see. Read Acts 10:38. The anointing of power is a healing and miracle anointing. Most people never see the power of God because they have not been anointed with power. The anointing of the Holy Spirit gives the inspiration and equipping for service, yet the anointing of power is what causes great miracles, signs and wonders. The anointing will only be released as you begin to do what you are anointed to do. You must be called and obey God in your calling, before you see the power displayed that God desires. The anointing of power is literally an anointing of God's actual power given to human flesh.

Jesus could feel the power to heal, leave his body. This is the anointing of power that can be imparted to bring healing and miracles by the laying on of hands. Many people have been healed in my ministry, when they weren't in faith and I wasn't in faith. It was just the anointing of power. When I would lay hands on them, the power would leave my body and enter them, healing them. I can't take any credit, it is just God's anointing of power to heal.

When I was attending Bible College, I had already pastored a church for a season. I was seeking God for him to confirm to me what he had called me to do and be.

I then had a vision on April 21, 1981. The Lord began to say in the vision "I have called you to be a prophet to the peoples of the world. You will go places here and there, you will go places here and there .. You will go there and start and establish a work there..." At the end of the vision he said "the reason I have caused you to have the vision is because of the janitorial work you have done …at the church."

I knew that God would keep sending me places here and

there. I also knew God had called me to be a prophet. I would later learn that a prophet is one that God gives revelations to, and the prophet is responsible before God to give that revelation. God will usually have prophets be writers or authors of books. Prophets were also required to pray for people, or it would be sin to them as it was for Samuel. This was part of the healing ministry. I was required as a prophet of God to pray for the sick. If I didn't do this, it would be a sin for me.

Some prophets in the Bible had schools, some were Pastors and some were prophets of politics. Yet these things were part of the prophet's ministry. Yet, God has a time for all things and we must wait for God's time. I learned you can get ahead of God or behind God's time. You must do things in the time that God wants it done.

In July 1982, I was at a "Camp Meeting" in Tulsa, Oklahoma. I was staying at my mother's home in Broken Arrow, Oklahoma. Shortly after I laid down, Jesus appeared to me. He was wearing a white robe. His hands were stretched out. I didn't see his face, but I knew beyond a doubt it was Jesus.

Then Jesus said, "Whatever you ask in my name, that will I do because I go unto the Father". The vision ended simple, scriptural, yet profound.

Jesus appeared and merely said what he said 2000 years earlier in John 14. Jesus had appeared six years later after my first experience with John 14, so I wouldn't forget that he still wanted me as a believer to be asking and doing the works that he did. Jesus wanted me to simply ask in this century, as he wanted people to simply ask 2000 years ago. He wanted me to be doing the works he did. He wanted me laying hands on the sick. He had anointed me for it. He wanted me to obey.

I have had many dreams and visions about healing, as

well as being healed myself. I want to share my favorite experience of the Lord healing me, and then I will share my favorite vision of healing.

I had a construction job going as I was pastoring a church. Somehow, I got something in my eye. I tried to get it out, but nothing seemed to work. It got so bad I had to get a man working for me, to drive my truck home and me as well. My vision was blurry, and I was beginning to have great pain.

I thought if I could go to sleep and when I awoke the next morning, it would probably have worked its way out.

The next morning my eyes were absolutely in great and terrible pain. The pain was devastating. I had thick drapes on my bedroom windows, yet the morning sun hurt my eyes, with my eyes closed. I had to cover my head because the light was creating great pain in my eyes. I couldn't open my eyes because of the intense pain.

I began claiming the promises of God, saying "I am healed by the stripes of Jesus, God sent his word to heal me and deliver me from destruction, Jesus himself took my infirmities" and other healing passages of scriptures, saying them over and over in my mind. I would then get out of bed and as an act of faith, force my eyes open. The pain was so great I would almost pass out. I did this twice, yet nothing happened.

I then remembered a story of a man in the book *The Game of Life and How to Play It.* There was a man who had broken his leg and he passed out three times, as he tried to claim his healing and walk as an act of faith. Three failures didn't stop him. The fourth time he tried to walk, he was completely healed.

I was determined to receive the healing that Jesus had for me, so I acted on my faith another time, in agony I fell back on the bed.

My mother came into my bedroom and said "Kyle, you

need to go to the emergency room of the hospital, your eyes are red and have bumps all over them".

I said, "I am healed by the stripes of Jesus, Jesus is my doctor, he took my infirmities". I then got out of bed, forcing my eyes open one more time. Instantly, miraculously, all redness, all the bumps, all the pain left. I was healed. My mother had seen the miracle happen, right in front of her eyes.

I have had countless dreams and visions of the blind being healed, people in wheelchairs being healed, and all kinds of healing and miracles. I have literally seen hundreds, or thousands of people being healed in dreams or visions, yet I stayed away from the healing aspect of ministry because people said I wasn't being balanced.

My favorite teaching vision regarding sickness happened in 1990. In this vision, I was aware of an unclean spirit. This spirit came toward me. I started to rebuke it, when the Lord said, "I want to teach you about the unclean spirit". I immediately knew I wasn't to resist this spirit, so God could teach me something.

In this vision, this spirit apparently entered my body, causing my eyesight to be blurred. I eventually became blind, my hearing began to fade away, and my voice began to only speak certain syllables. I couldn't pronounce words or sentences, only syllables. I eventually lost all control over my speech and lost my hearing. At this point I began to lose control over my body. My arms and body began to go in all different directions, uncontrollable. At this point I was blind, deaf, dumb, and had lost control over my body. I could not control any part of my body. I then began to lose control of my mind.

The Lord then said, "if it went any further, you would be possessed". I then regained control over my mind, my body, my hearing, my speech and my eyes. The Lord had taught me the lesson.

Unclean spirits can cause people to be blind, deaf, dumb, insane and to lose control of all or different parts of the body. I now knew that when one lost control of their mind, is when someone would be or become possessed. I immediately remembered the scriptures that showed Jesus giving the disciples power over unclean spirits when he sent them out to heal the multitudes.

The Lord had shown me, I had control or authority over these spirits. The unclean spirit could cause so many types of sickness and diseases. It was all scriptural. Yet is was an awesome experience. It was a vision, but I had all the experiences or feelings of being blind, deaf, dumb and no control over any part of my body. It was an awesome experience. It was an experience I don't think I will ever be able to forget.

Many people don't realize the spiritual realm that exists and sometimes controls the physical realm. We, through prayer and faith are to rebuke these spirits, so that physical circumstances change.

Many times, when people pray in tongues they will deal with these unseen forces as well. I have seen people healed just by praying in tongues and saying nothing in English. Praying in tongues is the most spiritual and powerful way to pray. Many people still have a lot of unbelief about the power of tongues.

I had one prophecy in a vision form. The prophecy was clear. I quote from the vision "tongues and preaching in the USA doesn't accomplish what it should, because of the unbelief that is in the USA". This was repeated twice in the vision. This was in 1995. The Lord wanted people to understand, it is and always has been unbelief that has stopped the effectiveness of preaching, but also tongues. People don't recognize the power that is to be realized by being faithful to pray in tongues.

In 1980 I was alone, praying in tongues at the altar of a church in Dallas. As I was praying in tongues, suddenly I saw a spirit. It looked like a monkey.

It was as if the only words that I knew would be effective were spirit words, or to speak against it in tongues. As I increased the intensity of tongues, it appeared to blow it away, or to cause this spirit to vanish. As I continued praying in tongues, I turned around and saw another spirit. It looked like a perverted kind of wolf. I increased praying in tongues to a greater intensity, like fourth gear, in spirit words or tongues, and suddenly, it was like it blew this spirit away as well.

Within two months this church went on daily television in the Dallas area. Was there a connection? I believe so, only God knows.

Yet, the spirit realm is very real. Spirit words, or tongues are needed to change the spirit realm. Spirits come and hinder churches and ministries. If the spirits aren't dealt with they can destroy anointed ministries, or at the least, keep them from fulfilling their potential.

I believe it was in 1986; I was living in Corpus Christi, Texas. KCTA Radio Station had given me a week's time on the radio, so I started praying about what to preach, and I heard an audible voice from the Lord.

He said, "I want you to go with A Time to Heal". I made the programs on the radio. Several people called and were healed. I still didn't quite realize that God wanted me to "Go" with healing.

That same week as I drove into a Quick Lube to get an oil changed on my truck, I met a man. This man, Mr. Davis, had heard me preaching on the radio. We talked about healing and rejoiced in some Christian fellowship.

He then said "my son, Steve, and a medical doctor, are going to Mexico to minister. Would you like to go with them and minister"?

I immediately started to say yes. Then I thought, I don't know this man. I don't know these people. They could be totally crazy. I told Mr. Davis that I would return the next day and tell him if I would go to Mexico. Well, within a few days, I was to go to Mexico. A man I had never met before arranged it. I was to meet two total strangers at 4 AM at a certain location. It would be dark. I would be alone. Yet, I had total peace about it.

I didn't have any money, so I borrowed $20 from a friend of mine. I wanted a little money to go to Mexico on. I knew God wouldn't let me down. I knew he would provide. I knew the Lord would protect me. So, in the middle of the night, I made my way to meet Steve Davis and Dr. Terry Elder. We eventually were on our way to Mexico.

We stopped at Harlingen to eat breakfast. A man came up and started talking as we were eating breakfast. He learned we were going down to Mexico to minister, so he took out some money and handed it, I believe to Steve. Steve said "no". But the man said, take it. I think it was Dr. Elder who said to give it to Kyle, he probably needs it. I had not told anyone that I didn't have any money, but God was faithful to provide.

We went to a village in the mountains in the central part of Mexico. God would do several things. This trip would begin a long relationship with Dr. Terry Elder, with Grace-Aire Medical Foundation. Also, many people would be saved and healed. Dr. Elder would have a medical clinic during the day, and at night we would preach and pray for the sick. Many people prayed to receive Christ. Within a few trips to the village, Dr. Elder and Steve would be responsible for almost everyone in the village receiving Christ. People are only saved because the Lord draws them, but if Steve and Terry

95

had not planned to go there, a whole village may have stayed lost and never received Christ.

It was in this village that I saw an interesting thing. A man had a short arm. There was a lot of confusion because of people wanting prayer. I wanted to command the arm to grow out in the name of Jesus, but Steve and Terry were talking to other people. They were my interpreters. I really didn't know if the Name of Jesus would work, if people didn't understand what I was saying or doing. To my amazement, as I spoke in English and commanded it to grow out, it did. The man didn't understand what I said, but the spirit realm responds to the Name of Jesus, and faith in Jesus' name in any language.

People with back problems and different things were healed. One man saw three moons. After ministering to him, he was healed and only saw one moon. I remember another lady couldn't read her Bible, but after prayer, she could read it. Probably 90% of the people were getting healed or dramatically improved immediately after prayer.

For me, the most interesting thing happened on the second trip to this same village. As we drove up to this village, some people started running up to the vehicle. They began to tell us this story.

This man had heard me preach and saw us pray for the sick. So, when his daughter was extremely ill, he remembered what was said. He went outside, up into the mountains. He prayed something like this: "I heard those men talk about you and your healing power. If you are real and will heal my daughter, I will commit my life to you". He then returned to his home. His daughter was healed. So, he then committed his life to Christ. He then went around to the surrounding villages telling what God had done.

Miracles will bring many people to Christ. Many people attack healing services because they don't realize that people need to see the supernatural power of God, to believe there is a God that is alive and powerful. I learned the principle of power evangelism from T. L. Osborn.

Suzanne Nouna and I, one night during 1981, decided to go street witnessing in Dallas. I started claiming the gift of healing and working of miracles, before we ever left. I wanted to demonstrate God's power to pimps and prostitutes, so they would receive Christ. To make a long story short, Suzanne and I had an appointment with a pimp at about 2 0'clock AM on a Saturday night. As we were talking to him, I asked him if there was anything wrong in his body, so I could pray for him.

He told me that he was shot once, and they could not remove the bullet. He said he had great pain in his leg.

I asked him if I could pray for him and he said that I could, but that I couldn't close my eyes, because he didn't want anyone to know he was being prayed for.

After I prayed I said to him, "begin to move your leg". He then had a surprised look on his face. God had healed him. He told us he had no pain, and what a miracle it was. I then lead him in a prayer to receive Christ.

As we left that night, he asked me to return the next day, so he could have his friends with him. The next night we returned. He only had one friend with him, but his place of business was closed. Power evangelism was truly the example of Biblical ministries.

When I was in Jamaica, I talked to many unsaved people. When they talked about being sick, they talked about going to what we would call, witch doctors, or spiritualists. They would go to these people instead of doctors, because they would pay with chickens and other things. They couldn't afford to go to doctors. I said, What about the churches? Why don't you go there and let people pray for you to be healed?

They looked completely confused as to why I would even

ask this question. The churches rarely saw anyone healed, so why would people go there for healing? People were going to witch doctors because the Church of Jesus Christ had lost the anointing of power to heal the sick. The church of the Bible was built on a healing ministry, but in the twentieth century, healings in churches rarely occurred.

It was because of some of my Jamaica experiences with people, witchcraft and demons that I saw a tremendous need to preach healing to the regions where witchcraft was so strong. They needed to have a healing alternative that didn't require money and doctors.

For several years, I prayed to have an avenue to preach healing on radio to some of these regions. I then discovered a radio station in the Caribbean that was heard in 21 Caribbean and South American countries. I kept praying about it until the Lord said to do it. I started in September of 1987, preaching healing on the radio every day. I didn't have any support, only a handful of people in the U.S. even knew about my ministry, but God was faithful.

I then stopped preaching about physical healing and started preaching healing of being backslidden, sin and bad habits. I concentrated on this for months. So, in June of 1988, I had to go off the radio station. I stopped focusing on physical healings, so the money stopped coming in. The radio station gave me grace, but it was years later before I learned that I must stay in the specific calling of anointing which I had, which was for physical healing.

I was sort of like Peter walking on the water. He wanted to do it, so Jesus said "come". Because Peter initiated the walking on water, not Jesus, his success would be conditional upon his faith. When Peter doubted, he began to sink.

I learned to always let the Lord be the one to tell me to do something. My good ideas and earnest desires, God will say yes to, but if I get out of faith or the specific anointing God wanted me functioning in, I would sink just as Peter did.

CHAPTER XIV

GO TO CHILE

In 1989 I was pastoring a church in Terrell, Texas that I had started, when the Lord told me he wanted me to leave the church. The Lord said it in what seemed like an audible voice. I began to pray about it.

I was just beginning to see some things happen and the church was growing, slowly, but growing. So, I began to seriously question whether it really was the Lord wanting me to go to.

After several weeks, I heard almost audibly "I want you to go to Chile". I now understood why the Lord wanted me to leave the Church. He wanted me to leave the church to go to Chile. I was just beginning to see a little prosperity and the Lord showed me I was to sell what I had and go to Chile.

I was even given a dream telling me that I needed to arrive in Chile before the end of February 1989. This would be my first trip to Chile or South America. In this dream, I was shown there would be some problems, but at the last minute, it would work out.

I had to sell my Mazda RX7. It was a fun car. I didn't want to sell it, but I had to obey God. I had to go to Chile. I had given away several vehicles at times and sold vehicles to do the work of the ministry, but my dune buggy and this Mazda RX7 were really sacrifices. It wasn't because they were so valuable, but because they were fun vehicles. Yet I knew I had to obey God.

I didn't know anyone in Chile. I didn't speak Spanish. Yet, God was sending me. I sent a letter to several friends of mine, hoping God would use it to bring in some more money, to help with this trip, but none came in from this.

I also seriously wanted my friends to pray, because I didn't know what to do or know anyone in Chile. So, I had asked them to pray for me.

A couple of days before I was to leave, a friend of mine contacted me. John Zieglar and I had worked together at Word of Faith Bible College. He was now working for Kenneth Copeland Ministries.

John called and said "I want you to come here to the ministry headquarters. I want you to meet Dr. Gonzales, he is from Chile."

Well, I borrowed a car, after all I had mine for sale at a car lot to sell. I went to Newark, Texas, the day before I was to leave to go to Chile. I met and enjoyed the fellowship with John, he is such a funny and gifted minister. John then introduced me to Dr. Gonzales, who was over most of the Spanish speaking ministers that had relationships with Brother Copeland.

Dr. Gonzales discussed several people that were involved in pastoral ministry in Chile. He then began to talk about Cliff Sanders, who was pastoring a church in Santiago. As he told me several things about Cliff, the Holy Spirit witnessed that this was the person I was to contact in Chile. Dr. Gonzales offered to write a letter of introduction for me.

I immediately said I would appreciate it. I then said goodbye to John and Ginger, John's wife. She was also working for

Brother Copeland. I drove back to Terrell rejoicing at the door God had opened.

I was to leave the following morning at 6 AM. I had almost no money, but my tickets were paid for, because Karl and Susan Morris gave me $1000 toward my ticket. Well, at 10 PM that night I finally had my car sold. I was only offered a percentage of what I thought the value was, so a friend of mine, Mark Mosser, said he would give me more money for it, but only $500 now, the rest later. I said that's fine, because I wanted to have some money to go to Chile on.

I arrived in Chile not knowing anyone. I couldn't count to ten in Spanish. I only had the post office box address of Cliff Sanders, but I had peace. I found a safe, decent, inexpensive hotel in the center of Santiago. I wrote a letter to Cliff and said where I was staying, so he could meet me or call me.

About two weeks later Cliff checked his post office box, so he contacted me. Cliff was serving as interim pastor at Renacer Christian Center. Rafael Martinez had started the church but had returned to the U. S. for a time. Cliff came to the hotel and picked me up. We went to church that night.

Cliff had a real pastoral gift and we immediately felt a witness in our spirits about helping each other. I didn't tell Cliff that I had almost no money when we met, but he offered to see if he could find a place to stay with someone in the church.

Angelica and Mariano Arancibia had an extra bedroom and volunteered their house. They wouldn't let me pay any money for it. This was great, for the day I left the hotel I only had enough money for a couple of days left. The Lord, as usual, was providing again.

I began preaching and ministering in Renacer Christian Center at least once a week. We were seeing some great miracles and things happening. Cliff finally received the letter from Dr. Gonzales and wanted to introduce me to some other pastors. Cliff was really impressed because of the miracles that he saw the Lord doing through me. So, he wanted to help other churches also experience these miracles.

One time, Cliff took me to a church. He knew the pastor and explained that Dr. Gonzales, working for Brother Copeland, wrote a letter of introduction to him in my behalf.

This other pastor wasn't too impressed about the Copeland connection, but as a favor to Cliff (I think), he started asking me what church I came out of. So, I explained my Word of Faith connection.

He said, "so Bob Tilton was your pastor". I said yes.

Immediately he became greatly offended at me, simply because of my previous church relationship. He was almost angry. Cliff tried to explain the miracles he had been seeing, but to no avail.

A woman came up saying she had been injured and had pain in her leg. I asked if I could pray for her, and she said yes. Well, the Lord healed her, as her pastor was standing there.

Yet, instead of his recognizing the healing anointing God had given me, I think he was even more offended, so we left.

The Lord used me as usual, to bring healing and salvation to many people. But any anointing should function outside the church meetings, as well as during church meetings. Because I believe this, I see many things happen not only in church services, but also out of the church.

One time at Renacer Christian Center I was greeting people as they came into the church. The service had started, but I was out by the street greeting people as they went by or came in. So, one man who had been drinking began to talk to me. I began to share Christ and later prayed with him to receive Christ. I then asked him to come into the church.

It was in Chile that I met my wife. Five years later, we would be married. As I was ministering at Renacer one night I saw her, and heard a little voice saying, "She will be your wife". I then started a relationship with her.

I always have many fond memories of Chile and the love that I experienced. I learned more about love from Angelica and Mariano Arancibia, and his parents Maria and Horaciao than from anyone in my life. As I stayed with them for months at a time during several visits to Chile, they became my family. I still love them as my own family.

As I continued ministering in Renacer, the original pastor, Rafael Martinez, and his family returned. His son, Denny, became a good friend and would also interpret for me at different places. Pastor Rafael was also impressed with the miracles he was seeing and compared me to Oral Roberts in the 1950's. All I can say, it is the anointing of God on my life.

I was praying one day in Chile and had a vision of a radio tower. I then remembered when I was in Jamaica, I had felt the Lord speaking to me that healing meetings were to be first, and then I would start radio stations. The radio station would help conserve the harvest of souls that received Christ. The radio station would serve as a Bible School, or as a 24-hour church to help strengthen these new believers.

I then began to pray about whether God wanted me to start a radio station in Chile. It was about this time that I received a letter that would open a whole new phase of ministry, eventually the radio ministry.

I had a dream about a black lady motioning for me to go a different direction. After prayer, I took this to mean the Lord was waiting for me to go in a different direction, to go to Africa. So, this dream started preparing me mentally to go to Africa.

Within a couple of days of this dream, I received a letter from Dr. Terry Elder. He said he had this great opportunity for me to go to Sierra Leone, West Africa. He also said that Jack Reed, T.L. Osborn's nephew would probably be going and be doing some miracle crusades for mass evangelism.

I wanted to learn how to hold miracle crusades, not the spiritual part as much as the technical aspects. I had been looking at places in Chile to start holding larger healing meetings. So, I thought this was the opportunity for me to learn a new phase of my healing ministry. I began seriously praying about going to Africa, after the letter from Dr. Elder. I had a witness in my spirit that I was to leave Chile and started preparing to go to Africa.

Jack Reed would decide to not go to Sierra Leone, but I still knew that God was leading me to go to Africa. The direction I had was from the Lord. So, I returned from Chile to start preparing for Africa. I didn't realize until three months later, that God would tell me to go to Sierra Leone and start a Christian Radio Station

CHAPTER XV

CULTURE SHOCK!

I returned to Terrell and began preparing and doing research about Sierra Leone. Sierra Leone was a country of over four million people in West Africa. In 1989, a U. S. Congressman had Sierra Leone as #1 on the world misery list. At that time, by some standards, Sierra Leone was the worst place to live in all the world. Reports of average life expectancy was between 37 and 41 years of age. This was a country in what was considered Moslem West Africa. The official language was English, so this would make ministry much easier.

I had met Baptist and Assembly of God missionaries that had said that Sierra Leone was the worst place to do anything in all of Africa. They said if I could do things there, I could do it anywhere in the world. Sierra Leone, they said, was a very, very difficult place. God was sending me to a place that had a reputation for being the worst place in the world, a place of extreme poverty, sickness, and about 90% illiteracy. The darkest place on the Dark Continent.

The Lord began to bring different people into my life, so I could learn about Sierra Leone before I went. One man who was a missionary for an "un-named" denomination, that told me that they didn't have a single native minister in their denomination that they could trust with money. Later he said they had found a few that they could trust in his denomination.

He also told me about much corruption and that bribery was a way of life. We began to hear stories of scams and swindles and how they were a way of life for many in Sierra Leone. Yet, despite this, I went very unprepared for what lay ahead.

Shannon Boettcher felt the leading of the Lord to also go to Sierra Leone with me. I will forever be grateful to him for his help and friendship. Shannon and I were preparing to go.

A person I will call Dr. Bzo, not his real name, was to be our official sponsor in Sierra Leone. The people in one church had asked Shannon and me to check up on or investigate Dr. Bzo. Dr. Bzo, of course, isn't his name, but because many things he did were illegal and immoral, I won't be using his real name.

As we prepared to go, Dr. Bzo was to be our government sponsor for Shannon and me in Sierra Leone. God used Dr. Bzo to help us, and to help get the first Christian Radio Station in Sierra Leone. God used him to do this and he should be honored for this, but because of many lies and fraud he committed, his name is obviously changed.

The names of many people mentioned in this book from this point on have had to be changed for obvious reasons.

The Lord finally spoke in October of 1989, saying to go to Sierra Leone and start a Christian Radio Station. I knew it was finally time to begin a radio station and that the place of starting the first radio station would be Sierra Leone.

The weekend before we left the USA, I was holding a three-day healing meeting in Terrell, Texas. During this meeting, $178,000 was pledged to the ministry to help with

Africa.

Dr. Elder and Bruce Tyler had paid for Shannon's and my tickets to Africa. God was truly showing that this was of him. As we were preparing to go, I made a trip to South Texas, where I visited Dr. Elder, and Bob and Doris Bush.

While we were in South Texas, we spent two days in South Padre Island, Texas. I there had two dreams that showed I was to call people to help the ministry, that God had called people to support the ministry and I needed to call them to a place of commitment to give and help the ministry. God was calling me to teach giving so the ministry wouldn't lack.

As we left the U. S. we knew we were in the will of God, and God was with us.

Later, because it would take several years to start the station, only about $3,000 out of the pledged $178,000 was ever given. Yet, because people had pledged this, when government leaders asked about where my financial support would come from to do the station, I boldly quoted the amount pledged. This $178,000 that was pledged and never paid, helped us gain favor with some government officials. Now I can see God's hand in it, but for several years it was a point of bitterness in me that I had to repent and forgive the people that promised money and never gave it.

Shannon and I finally arrived in Freetown, Sierra Leone. When we arrived at the airport, everyone was wanting money. Dr. Bzo wasn't there but had someone at the airport take us to his house.

On the way into Freetown from the airport, we began to see a city and people who were in greater poverty and dirtier, than any I had seen in Mexico, the Caribbean, or South America. The previous experiences never really prepared me sufficiently for the poverty of Sierra Leone. People from all over the world would come and say it was the worst they had seen, worse than Haiti, worse than Mexico, worse than India. Yet, God had sent us to this place.

You must cross the harbor to get into Freetown. There was no bridge, so you must take a ferry. Well, I had been on ferries before, but none as old as this. When you drove on in one direction, you would have to back the car out the same side you drove in on. It was crazy. Shannon and I laughed, because it was such a crazy looking thing for us. But it was business as usual for the Sierra Leoneans.

We would discover a few weeks later that the Japanese had given Sierra Leone the money to purchase two ferries, but those in charge pocketed the money and painted the old ferries. It was just standard practice for Sierra Leone.

As we made our way in to Freetown, we discovered the Capitol City only had electricity a few hours a week. The generators were old and worn out. You felt lucky or blessed if you had electricity eight hours during an entire week.

We finally met Dr. Bzo, and he extended apologies for not meeting us at the airport. He then took us to a nice hotel where he and "Mr. Frederick" arranged for our rooms. We had to pay for the hotel, but it was at a discount rate. We were very glad to have a clean hotel room. The hotel had a generator, so we had continuous electricity.

Praise God. After months with little or no electricity, you come to greatly appreciate lights and every electrical appliance that you have ever used.

We soon discovered that no one could call out of the country. It was November 1989, yet it was impossible to make a phone call out of the country. The official government response was that a fire had damaged the equipment. Other sources told us that the government refused to pay for the satellite time, or the government- controlled phone company didn't pay its telephone bill and eventually was told, it could not access the satellites to make phone calls until they paid their bills. I was told eventually that the E.U. countries paid for it. Regardless of why, no one could make a long-distance phone call for about a month. This was truly the dark continent. Within weeks we would learn many things about the country, the people, the government, and the culture. We would learn much about the corruption that was reportedly going on in the government.

One man told us that he had brought a ship load of rice to Sierra Leone. He had a contract for it to be sold for $6 a bag upon arrival in Freetown. The man he had a contract with knew certain government officials who impounded the ship. The man couldn't take his ship out of the port because the man wanted to pay only $3 a bag for the 100 pound bags of rice. Eventually, the owner of the ship was told how to get the ship out of port. The owner told me how he had to pay $70,000 to a court judge before he could take his ship out of port. The ship was stuck in Freetown for about three months. He had lost several hundred thousand dollars.

We would soon hear of first-hand accounts of so much corruption in the government, that we knew people in the U. S. could not believe any country in the world could be so corrupt. We would read the newspapers and laugh because of the extreme corruption that was obvious, and even openly published in the newspaper. Yet, nothing was done about the extreme corruption. I had thought Mexico was a corrupt country, until I went to Sierra Leone. The government of Mexico was almost a saint by comparison. It was truly unbelievable. Words could never explain the depths of corruption. Other government leaders I would talk to over the next several years explained why.

The people in the government were getting paid such a small amount, that they would go to work every day trying to figure out some way to provide for their family. They had to get money in some way. The bribery and corruption were the only way many people could buy food for their families. To show you how bad it was, in 1989 the president's official salary was just a little over $1000 a year. Everyone else received far less. Most people received only about $30 per month.

I saw the government payroll charts which showed what everyone in the government was getting paid. The reason for the corruption was simple. The people in the government were not getting a living wage, they were getting paid less than it takes to live. How can you expect people to be honest, when they don't receive a living wage? When I understood this, I could understand, but not condone, their corruption and bribery. I could then walk in love and mercy to these government officials.

We then began to start taking trips up country, or to the interior of Sierra Leone. There would be military check points along the way, to every place you wanted to go up country. These check points would be very intimidating. Armed men with machine guns would have the roads blocked. We had to stop while the soldiers checked us out and the vehicle we were in. If you didn't give them anything, then you must pray for favor. After a while this can become a very trying experience.

After a couple of months of this, Shannon got mad. He wanted to tell off these soldiers. Shannon is one of the quietest persons you will ever meet, but after a while it even got to him. As he was fixing to really let one soldier have it, I said "Shannon, this is Africa, not the U. S. Here they can kill you and take your body into the bush (or jungle) and no one can do anything about it". It brought him back to the Sierra Leone reality.

There were many situations to overcome. Most of the women out of the capital city of Freetown, wore no clothes above their waist. After a time, you literally see thousands of women's bare breasts. People who can't handle this, sure don't need to go to Africa. Some of the young girls are very proud of their breasts. They go around strutting, showing off their breasts in front of everyone. It is nothing to see people bathing beside a street or road. There is much male and female nudity throughout Africa.

The young girls will try to get pregnant, so they can get someone to marry them, and begin to help take care of them. It is quite different from American culture.

We would also begin to learn about the secret societies, or witchcraft societies. Because Dr. Bzo's father was the head of one of the secret societies, we could see and experience many things that few Americans ever get to see. Dr. Bzo and his father both received money from denominational churches in the U. S., yet Dr. Bzo's father was one of the most respected Juju men, or witch doctors in Sierra Leone. When his name was mentioned in the first Vice President's office, it immediately got respect. God uses unusual circumstances sometimes.

One day we were to go to one of the primitive rituals that few outsiders ever see. We were already in a very remote place, but this day we drove down a road that obviously had not been used in years. We crossed a bridge that required us to get out of the truck and help fortify the bridge before we could cross. We finally arrived at an extremely remote village.

There we were met by the dancing of the devil. One person dressed as a jungle devil and has names written on him. The ritual devil dancing continues for hours. We acted as though we were totally stupid about that was going on, because we never contradicted their explanations of what was happening but showed expressions of approval and interest. We have seen what few ever tell about.

As the ritual dances continued, the devil came and took a baby away from a mother. The baby was screaming as the devil takes it in his body. The devil then took the baby to an altar. There was an altar of sacrifice, that this devil uses to offer sacrifices on. As he put the baby on the altar, the devil then took a knife, as if he was going to a kill the baby in sacrifice. They didn't kill the baby while we were there, yet they said they were just showing us this ritual. We left before the sun went down. The ritual continued for another eight and a half hours after we left. We could hear the ritual drums beating throughout the night. We were both sure that with the real ritual, the baby would be sacrificed by the "devil" to another devil that was stronger and more powerful than he was. This was all a part of the secret society that rules many countries in Africa.

Mr. Bzo, who was an active member and head of a secret society, but also a pastor of a church, he told us that there were far more human sacrifices under Islam, than there were with the secret societies. The Moslems in certain sects would offer human sacrifices, per the seven books of Moses. Both secret societies and sects within the Moslem religion offered human and animal sacrifices to obtain prosperity, obtain political office and to obtain desired things.

One story that was in the local newspaper went something like this. A man wanted to be elected town chief. Apparently, his juju man, or witch doctor told him he needed to sacrifice a young virgin, so he could get elected. The man found a lady that wanted to sell her niece for $40 U.S. They killed the girl in the jungle, performed the ritual sacrifice, and then cooked the body with Plantain and rice. (Eating the sacrifice would help insure the benefits of the sacrifice were received).

The police discovered what happened, because the lady who sold her niece, went to the police to get the police to make the man pay the $40 to her. After the girl was sacrificed, the man never paid the woman. Therefore, the police accidently discovered what happened.

Not only is animal and human sacrifice common, but some people like to eat human flesh. A good friend of mine told me the following story that happened in his town.

A woman was a trader that deals with babies. She would kidnap babies and children. She would then sell them to people who would take them to Arab countries, or people who needed to make a sacrifice. One day the police found her as she was cooking three babies in a 55-gallon barrel. They arrested her, but later she was released after a reported bribe.

Everyone in the town knew of her desire to eat babies, as well as selling babies. Out of her guilt and as her offering apparently to God, she built and paid for a Moslem Mosque to be built in the town. Because everyone knew this Mosque was built with blood money, everyone wanted to stay away from this Mosque. She still lives in the town and feared by the people.

During one period in Sierra Leone, per reports told me by two people who worked for the Sierra Leone Intelligence, every time people would build a Moslem Mosque, there would be an animal sacrifice and a human sacrifices buried under the Mosque, to insure the success of the Mosque.

Another good friend of mine told me of a lady who wanted political power. Her juju man, or witch doctor, told her she needed to sacrifice her own child and bury the child under her desk in her office. She has power in one chiefdom and several people know how she sacrificed her own child to get it. She continues to believe the sacrifice of her child is continuing to give her wisdom to be successful in the chiefdom politics.

One paramount chief told me, "The Christian's God is merciful; The Moslem's God is merciful, but the devil shows no mercy, so we serve him.

One diamond dealer who was later forced to leave the country told us the following personal experience.

"Zanutoo" wanted to be able to get diamonds, so he began to do all the cultural things of sacrifice, blood covenants, and the like. After a period, he was finally initiated into one of the secret societies.

Of course, when you make the blood covenant, it is a covenant with the people of the society, and indirectly with the devil. If you tell people what goes on in the society, you will be killed. Zanutoo said if anyone found out what he was fixing to tell us that he would be killed. Several others who told me stories of the secret societies said they would be killed as well, if anyone found out that they had told us certain things.

Zanutoo explained that after he was initiated, he was made a full member of this one secret society. This gave him all the rights and privileges of the society. He said twice a year in this secret sect, the covenant principle would be in effect. (The covenant principle is anything that one person has must be shared with anyone else that wants to use it). For one week, twice a year, the people in this secret society could trade furniture and use anything of those in the society. It was so extreme that if one person wanted to have sex with anyone else in the society, no one could say no. Husbands, wives, fathers, mothers, sons and daughters could not say no. No one could say no to anyone else who was in the society, if they wanted sex with someone.

Zanutoo liked this aspect of the society because he liked having sex with the different people. He explained the different secret societies have different rules, and different guidelines. Zanutoo wasn't a Christian, yet he helped us on several occasions.

Along the way, I met Ben Tipton, an Assembly of God Missionary. He shared several things that helped me in dealing with the secret societies. He also told of some African leaders who had "juju men", or "witch doctors" as their political advisors. I had heard from other sources as well, about human and animal sacrifices that many heads of state in Africa had made, in their equivalent of the White House. He shared some personal encounters he had with these people and explained when these "witch doctors" are confronted with the name of Jesus and boldly challenged, they lose their power. These juju men, or witch doctors, often lose their miraculous or supernatural power when confronted with the power of the Living God.

Well, Ben and his crusade team were trying to get ten to twenty churches started in Sierra Leone, when an unusual thing happened. Ben had been preaching in this village in a tent.

After he left, a native evangelist came to preach. They had a sound system, so many people could hear everything the preacher said. This native evangelist began to tell the secrets of the secret society. He began to tell how they would do things to make people think it was supernatural, when in fact it was nothing supernatural at all.

As the native evangelist began to deal with specific secrets, the local men of the secret society began to get the members of the society together. They were going to come and kill the native evangelist. A man who knew Ben, came and told the evangelist to leave immediately because they were coming to kill him. The man left.

The secret society, which also controlled the Chiefdom Court had the pastor of this new church arrested. The following day, some Assembly of God officials came down to the village to get the pastor released and to try to resolve the situation. The Chiefdom Court released the pastor on the condition that the Assembly of God officials bring this evangelist back to the village to stand trial at 10 AM the following Saturday morning.

So, the following Saturday, the church officials returned

to the village with the evangelist, but they left the evangelist waiting in a car outside of the village. As they arrived, the Chiefdom Court had met and had already passed sentence. The evangelist was to die for violating sacred traditions. They were there waiting with machetes to kill the evangelist when he arrived, but he never arrived.

A different missionary of the Assembly of God denomination told me the following story. A man working for this missionary had received Christ. He later started to go to Bible college.

The man who had received Christ we will call "John". John told the missionary that his family would kill him. He said before they kill me, I must try to lead some other people in my family to Christ. In the Moslem Sect that his family was in, they would give him some time to come back to the Moslem religion. If he did not return to the Moslem religion, then his family apparently could kill him, and he could still be saved, at least according to their beliefs.

Several weeks after the man left the missionary, his body was found floating in the river. He was found with a stake driven through his tongue, because he confessed with his mouth the Lord Jesus.

The missionary later learned the dead man did lead his mother to the Lord, before he was killed. The mainline Moslem denominations do not practice these types of things. However, the fringe elements of Islam are often ruling the Moslem religion in Africa.

I have seen Islamic preachers or Imams have the children attending one of the Moslem schools, line up outside the school. They would then give them money, so everyone could see the money that the Moslems had. The Moslems lead many people astray because of their prosperity message.

These are some of the stories that can help you understand

the circumstances and cultural conditions in which we were going to start the first Christian radio station in Sierra Leone.

CHAPTER XVI

AFRICA - PHASE I

The Lord had said to go to Sierra Leone and start a radio station, so I would be ministering in churches, usually up country in the provinces, and then be returning to Freetown, the capitol city, to deal with the government officials. Over the period of several years, I would have several hundred meetings with government officials before we would gain all the necessary approvals.

When we arrived in the country, we registered with the U. S. Embassy/Consulate, and they told me we should contact the Ministry of Information and Broadcasting and talk to the Minister (secretary) of Information and Broadcasting. I started to learn of the politics that goes in on all of the countries of the world. I do jokingly tell people I went as a preacher and returned as a politician.

Dr. Bzo, Shannon and I went and met the Minister of Information and Broadcasting. He explained what we officially needed to do. This was December 1989. In April 1993, we would finally have every approval needed, without paying a bribe to anyone to obtain the permits.

I prepared a 13-page document outlining in detail our plans

for a radio station that would include international shortwave transmitters as well as a local transmitter. I would present our plans to the President's office, the First Vice President's office, the Minister of Information and Broadcasting, as well as the Minister of Health, Rural Development, and Social Services, Education, Industry and Trade, Power, Mines, and Transportation and Communication. I would personally meet with most of the top leaders of the nation.

President Momoh was the President at the time. His office sent a letter of recommendation to the Ministry of Information and Broadcasts recommending quick approval of our proposed projects. I didn't understand much of African politics, so when the Permanent Secretary asked me who I knew in the president's office, I said no one, it is just the Lord doing it. I would later learn that I should have just said "a friend" and be referring to the Lord.

When we went to the First Vice President's office, we were not really being received until Dr. Bzo tried to explain who his father was (without us understanding what he was talking about). As soon as he realized that Mr. Bzo was Dr. Bzo's father, immediately he wanted to help. The secret society connections are about the strongest connections you can have in the worldly realm in Africa. In the end, these connections did not help any, but it was interesting to see how it would normally work.

As I continued playing politics and visiting all the cabinet members who must approve the permits, I was sent a message. One cabinet minister sent word for me to meet with him because he wanted to tell me how much it would cost (bribe) to get our approval. I told the man who brought the message, "I am not going to meet with him because I am not going to pay a bribe". God had told me to do this, so God was going to have to do it without a bribe.

One of the approvals I got the first time I was in Africa

was funny. The ministry kept saying they approved of our project but would never give an official letter confirming the approval. So, I told the Permanent Secretary I was going to have to return to the U. S. And needed something in writing to show people in the U. S. that I had been doing something. The Permanent Secretary told me to write out a letter and he would sign it. So, I wrote out a letter, he made some minor changes in it, then he had it typed on an official letterhead. He signed it and sealed it. Without realizing it, he had given us one of the approvals we needed. I didn't have to pay a bribe, but I received this approval without him even realizing it until several days later. I made copies of his approval and sent it to other departments or ministers, so they could see that others were giving their approval as well.

I thought the P.S. would be angry with me for playing a trick on him, but he only laughed and respected me for getting it in the manner in which we received it. In their culture if you can trick someone into doing something, they respect you because you must be more intelligent than they are. To me it was just the Grace of God.

This was a place to learn great patience. I would have appointments with government leaders and must wait for hours to see them. One man made me wait for four days outside of his office before he would finally see me. I had an appointment for 9 am on a Monday, I got to meet with him that Friday at 3pm. I would learn that you would wait until you gave someone some money. Since I wouldn't give the money, I would have to wait a long time.

Then there is also B.M.T., or black man time. One day Dr. Bzo was to pick us up at 9 AM. At 1 PM he finally showed up. He explained that it was 9 AM B.M.T. which most knew meant any time after 9. We would later learn lots of black and white people would commonly refer to being late as B.M.T. or black man time. This, of course, came from the village culture where time really wasn't important.

Learning any culture is necessary to gain success but learning how to play politics was fun and funny. The political culture in Africa basically would be summed up by saying everyone wants something and if you show them you want to help them, they will usually want to help you. The problem is most wanted the help of money for themselves personally, not just the help and progress of their country, children or village.

Since I was learning how to play politics, I was beginning to get some of the privileges of having friends in high places. One of the greatest privileges was being able to purchase gasoline at the official $2 a gallon price. Up country there was always gasoline shortages which would cause the unofficial price for gasoline to climb to about $10 a gallon. One paramount chief always helped us get gasoline. There could be 100 people waiting to get gasoline and officially they wouldn't have gasoline to sell, but a word from the paramount chief and we would always get gasoline at the official price. Many times, people were amazed at how we could get gasoline when no one else could.

There was much sickness and disease also to overcome. Sierra Leone and West Africa were called the white man's grave. They have problems I had never heard of anywhere. There is a bacterium that can get in your skin. This bacterium then begins to grow in your skin until a worm or worms start to crawl out of your skin. Of course, there is malaria, which causes your brain to swell and start to hemorrhage. Shortly after we arrived, an American died of a brain hemorrhage due to malaria. Shannon and I also contracted the malaria virus. Once my brain felt as if it was about six feet wide and about to explode, but the Lord healed me. Shannon would eventually go back to the states for medical reasons, a severe case of malaria.

One person's testicles turned blue due to an African

sickness. When the person told me, his testicles had turned blue, I told him to forget about the doctors in Sierra Leone and return to the U. S.

While I was there I was bitten by an acid fly that injects acid under the skin. It took about three months before the skin grew back and returned to its normal color.

There are also biting river flies that cause blindness, I was bitten by those as well.I was fishing at one of the rivers when I looked down at my legs. I had on my swim suit. There were spots of blood all over my legs. The biting river flies eat your skin, but you can't feel them on you or feel it when they bite you, but they eat the skin until you start to bleed. Then they lay their larvae there. The larvae of the biting river fly then enters your body. As I looked down I was shocked to see myself bleeding, yet I felt nothing. This happened on several occasions, yet by the Grace of God, and without medication, I have never become blind because of the biting river flies.

Since I was raised in the country, in Texas, I didn't worry about swimming in the river with snakes or alligators in Africa. We would sometimes be in ponds with a water moccasin swimming a few feet away from us, but I never dreamed this experience would help prepare me to be a missionary in Africa.

I was asked to preach in a Methodist Church. I prepared a message that nothing was too hard for God. After the message, I began to pray for people with back problems. All that came forward said they were healed or dramatically improved. The Paramount Chief's arm grew out about 4 inches. I then gave an altar call for salvation. No one came forward to receive Christ.

I was asked to preach there the following Sunday, so I really began to pray about what to preach. The miracles usually caused people to receive Christ. This time no one wanted to receive Christ after seeing miracles. I knew I must go with a different message and a different type of ministry. So, the following week, I really prayed for the right message.

The next Sunday morning I preached on eternal judgement. When I gave, an altar call this time, 90% came forward to receive Christ or repent from sin. That night we would go to the river and baptize, if I remember it correctly, 26 people.

My desire in baptizing the people was to be scriptural, but Dr. Bzo decided it would be good to raise funds if he had a video tape of baptizing people in the water. So, after we left, he got a number of people together and video taped people getting baptized. He then sent this to the people in the U. S. To raise funds.

If he was truly interested in people getting saved, I wouldn't have a problem with his video-taping water baptism, but Dr. Bzo had sound equipment from churches that he used to operate a discotheque and sell beer and hold dances. He would use this equipment bought and donated to help the gospel ministry, to promote the work of the devil. He was involved in adultery, smuggling, and fraud. His Mercedes was bought in Belgium with money sent to buy a truck for agricultural uses. He promoted the secret society and openly said every person that ever became rich started out with a crime. This was a so-called "Christian Minister". This was a minister we were asked to investigate by a church in the U. S.

I would eventually leave Africa the first time without obtaining the permits. Yet, many people had received Christ. We had planted gospel seeds with many people. We had survived the first experience in Africa. The political process was started. Churches and Christians in Sierra Leone were praying for a Christian radio station. I had shared the vision for the station in Wesleyan, Methodist, Assembly of God and independent churches. There were many influential people, but especially Princess James, that were helping with prayer and political contacts.

Before I would leave, I was robbed. I had cashed a check at one business. This businessman's partner had me followed. While I was at a restaurant, two men created a diversion while one took my briefcase. I noticed it almost immediately after the diversion. We ran out the door to catch the thief, but they were too quick.

The owner of the Rooster Restaurant in Freetown was very gracious about the robbery, for he bought me a new briefcase.

Yet my checkbook, passport, and important government letters were stolen. Over the next several months, there would be over $10,000 U. S. Dollars in forged checks written on the ministry account.

Since the checks were cashed in Korea, London, Hong Kong, and San Francisco, I knew who was behind the theft, but I could do nothing. It was the son-in-law of the head of one of the denominations in Sierra Leone. This man was trying to sell me stolen cars from Europe, even as he had to the denomination of his father-in-law. The denomination bought them as new, and the father-in-law pocketed the difference. This man was involved in business endeavors in all the places the checks were cashed and deposited, yet his father-in-law was the head of a denomination.

Welcome to Sierra Leone, a place in need of true gospel preached by true people of God. A place of adventure and danger. A place of darkness that needed the light of the gospel.

CHAPTER XVII

A CHALLENGING AND EXCITING ADVENTURE IN

AFRICA, THE SECOND JOURNEY

My second trip to Africa would come after much controversy and after I had basically given up on the station.

When I reported my findings about Dr. Bzo to the U. S. Church, they did nothing but cover up the problem. Since I had promoted Dr. Bzo in my newsletters and my home church, I felt I had an obligation to generally disclose what Dr. Bzo had done. I felt this was the scriptural thing to do. So, I explained the specific fraud, theft, and history of the man.

Was I surprised!! This was during a period in the U. S. where everyone was saying the Christians should police their own ministries and churches. I was, in my opinion, taking part in a policing action. I was merely trying to stop abuses of a certain minister. But after the policing action, no one other than my home church gave anything to the ministry for over a year. Dr. Bzo continued receiving money from people because his organization would do nothing to expose or stop his abuses. The only one who was ever financially affected was me. This taught me to say nothing about many of the abuses I would see over the next few years. I would sometimes contact people in their organizations, but only one time did an organization do something to change or stop the abuses that missionaries or ministers were involved in. They had their doctrines of accountability, but they didn't want people to lose credibility and therefore the giving to missions to stop.

After my report about Dr. Bzo, and not easily getting the permits, many people began to question if the station was of God. I began to believe it really wasn't God, but God began to give me dream after dream, and even prophesies about the station that would happen in Sierra Leone.

I received a letter from Dib Shahine saying he believed if I returned to Sierra Leone that I would be able to obtain the permits. Dib was Princess James' relative by marriage, and since I had some confidence in Princess James, I decided to pray about returning to Africa.

When I started praying about returning, I learned that Dr. Bzo was telling people that if I returned, I would be killed, or at the least,arrested, and put in prison. I told some friends in my home church about the threats on my life, so they could be praying.

I then received a prophecy saying if I returned to Sierra Leone I would be killed. Despite the prophecy and the threats, I decided to go to Sierra Leone. After much prayer, I knew it was God's will for me to go.

One friend of mine said, "we will know if the prophecy was of God. If you return, we will know it wasn't of God. If you are killed, we will know the prophecy was of God". Several friends of mine said that I wasn't walking in wisdom and left my home church in protest because in their eyes, I was wrong about going to Africa.

In February 1992, with only a handful of people standing in faith with me, I left to go to Africa. About half the people had left my small home church during my year of controversy.

I would only have about five people who would give to me or the ministry because of the loss of credibility during the worst year of my life. This was a trying of my faith; it was unlike anything I had ever experienced.

Veronica, who I would marry several years later, rejected me and said no, after she had said yes, and after I had told everyone on my mailing list I was going to Chile to get married. I arrived in Chile, and Veronica's mother said she would kill herself if we got married. So, Veronica canceled our wedding plans. When I returned to the U. S. without a wife, after saying I knew it was the will of God, people were convinced I was a false prophet at the worst, or I didn't recognize the voice of God, at the best.

With failing to obtain the permits in Africa, and the failing to get married to Veronica, even I had great doubts of my calling and my ability to follow God. 1991 was the worst year of my life, but it didn't stop me. I left to go to Africa.

I had to stay over in France for several days before I would go down to Sierra Leone. I called Celia Bonds and she picked me up at the airport. Shirley Crosby was staying at the house as well as another lady. Since they were all intercessors, I told them to pray for the station and what I felt God wanted me to do. I also told Celia to pray for my finances, because I had less than $100 to go to Africa on.

Before I left Paris, France, Shirley Crosby gave me the offering that Celia's church had given Shirley for ministering at her church. So, I could leave Paris with less than $200, not a lot, but enough to legally enter the country of Sierra Leone.

When I arrived at the hotel, I only had enough money for two nights, so I paid for one night and went to my room.

After I took a shower and was in bed with only my underwear on, a prostitute came in. She had a key to my room, and came right in. I told her to leave. I was glad that she left quickly, because she was a very pretty lady. I knew my resistance to a sex sin was low because of all the rejection I had experienced that year. But God is faithful and would not allow me to be tempted above what I could resist. I resisted the sin, but if she had persevered, I know I would have fallen into a sin. I spiritually was weak, and I knew it.

I finally met with Dib, and he invited me to stay at his house. Since I had no money, I quickly said yes. I stayed at Dib's house for the next few months. Dib's house had no air conditioning and had electricity only about 8 hours every week. Yet, I was so glad to have a place to stay. Dib said I could just pay whatever I felt like paying. It was really a blessing.

One of the first things I did was to register with the U. S. Embassy and tell them about the threats of being killed or being put in prison. I told them about investigating Dr. Bzo, and who would be responsible for my death if I was killed within the next few weeks. They thought I was crazy for coming but understood the martyr missionary mentality.

After establishing contact with the U. S. Embassy, I went to a friend of mine in the Ministry of Industry and Trade. As I went to his office, a cabinet member, the Minister of Housing was in his office. I began to explain what I had been told, and why some bad rumors were being told about me. The Ministry of Housing then began to say that he had heard that I was coming back to Sierra Leone to overthrow the country.

As most people know, in a third or fourth world government, rumors of this kind can get you killed or put in prison. The cabinet minister said he was glad to have met me and to know the whole story. He also began to help me correct some of the lies that were being told about me.

There was also a high-ranking military official trying to convince people I was returning to be smuggling gemstones.

What the General didn't know was that I had taken some mineral samples of corundum, which is rubies and sapphire. The Ministry of Mines gave some to me. I had them and others analyzed and looked for a market for the commercial grade corundum. President Momoh had a letter in his files about them, as well as a prominent Paramount Chief and the Ministry of Mines.

This trip, I had tangible information about minerals in the country that few people in the government knew. Instead of giving bribes, I would now tell about these rubies and sapphires that were in the country. This helped me gain the favor of many government officials who later helped me. I had a means of helping the people. I personally never made one dollar off gemstones in Africa, but God used this to help gain favor.

The general who was telling lies about me would eventually be overthrown and not be able to return to Sierra Leone without being arrested. My righteousness would answer for me in time to come.

How I came to learn about gemstones was from a friend, Forrest McMillan. He knew about the diamonds in Sierra Leone. He tried to get me to take some books about the diamonds and gemstones, but I refused. When I arrived in Sierra Leone, almost everyone talked about diamonds. I knew absolutely nothing about diamonds, and felt stupid, being in a country that almost everyone talked about diamonds. Out of a desire not to feel stupid, I had Forrest send me two books. With these two books, I got to know more technical information about gemstones than 99% of the people in Sierra Leone. I would try to give the information to the Sierra Leone people and Christians.

I saw that they were being financially raped through their ignorance and wanted to help by giving them information so they, could regain control over the economy and their lives.

Within a couple of months, many knew the lies and the truth, and I was able to gain favor with people, even in the intelligence community. One of the top intelligence persons asked me to work with Sierra Leone Intelligence.

The U. S. Counsel told me some guidelines of how to do things so I would not be legally liable or have problems, but he thought it was good because it showed that they had confidence in me.

Sierra Leone Intelligence personnel later said if I would help them identify the sincere ministers from the fraudulent, that they would help me get the permits for the radio station. I never really did much with them, but I had one very interesting experience.

I asked a friend to help me find out what the government had to be afraid of. I was talking about us, getting the permits for the radio station. He misunderstood, an interpreted it to mean what did the government have to be afraid of.

A week later he told me about a man who had overthrown 21 countries and was coming to Sierra Leone to overthrow it. I was told who he was, his name was John Barnes, and I thought it couldn't be true. I was making jokes about it, but I did tell some friends who worked with an intelligence agency. I never thought for a moment that it was true. This was on a Sunday.

The following Thursday I was out at the hotel drinking my Coke, when the Sierra Leone intelligence man came up to where I was sitting. He always was drinking a beer and smoking a cigar, if he was at this hotel. But this time he sat down beside me, put his cigar out and ordered a cup of tea. He then started the conversation by saying "I don't want you to think you are in trouble or anything, but how did you know about the man who was coming to overthrow the country. You see, we arrested him at the airport today. Scotland

Yard had him under surveillance and when he left England, British Intelligence followed him and notified Sierra Leone Intelligence that he was coming to Sierra Leone.

I told how I came to have the information.

This man who had come to Sierra Leone had been a former British Intelligence officer. But after he left them, he worked for whoever would pay him. He would come to a new government and have fake CIA documents, or false British Intelligence documents. He would then overthrow the government by giving them false information. He would overthrow the government by causing them to distrust the loyal, and trust the disloyal, or those who were paying. Using this method, he had overthrown 21 countries from within.

There were some interesting adventures spiritually as well. I had a daily program about physical healing on the radio. There were two radio stations, the government and ABC radio. I bought some radio time for a daily radio program. This opened the door to ministry opportunities, but most importantly, I was fulfilling the perfect will of God and abiding in his protection.

I was at a missionary fellowship that discussed how a man had challenged all the witch doctors. As they were talking about a historical event, something clicked inside of me, I thought I should do this.

I prayed about it and had my faithful few pray -about me challenging all the witch doctors, juju men, or anyone claiming to have spiritual power in the country.

I used my radio program to challenge these people, such as juju men, to kill me with supernatural means. I told them that they couldn't because of the blood of Christ and my faith in him. I made a five-minute recording of my challenge to be played on the radio station every day. I played the challenge every day for a week. I gave the deadline for Saturday, 5 PM.

I mocked the juju man, the witch doctors and other people that kept so many Sierra Leoneans in fear. I openly challenged and mocked them on radio. I did this as one that has the power over them as simply a Christian.

I was having a Coke and a donut at Crown Bakery when I met Dr. Robert Smith, with the Red Sea Mission, Sudan Interior Mission, minister in the Church of Scotland, and lecturer at Furah Bay College. He recognized my voice from radio. He said he only knew two other people, Eric Cowely and Russ Tatroo, who would have enough boldness and faith to issue a challenge like that. He said he was praying for me and standing with me. We would eventually become good friends.

Well, the witch doctors and the juju men were not able to kill me. One Christian, in faith can withstand every spiritual attack of all the witch doctors combined. The Lord was my refuge and my fortress. The Lord proved faithful.

I would eventually meet Mrs. Gooding, through Russ Tatroo, who would help us greatly with the radio station. Eric Cowley, a powerful evangelist leading many crusades, would also eventually become a friend. God was continually causing me to be at the right place at the right time, to meet who he wanted me to meet.

One night about 2 0'clock in the morning, I heard a man in the compound scream and take off running. This woke me up.

I immediately prayed Psalm 91:2 - I WILL SAY OF THE LORD HE IS MY REFUGE AND MY FORTRESS; MY GOD, IN HIM WILL I TRUST. I then rolled over and went back to sleep.

I had no idea what was going on until about an hour later, Dib knocked on my bedroom door saying "Kyle, are you okay"? I awoke and said "yes, why?"

Four men armed with AK47's had come into the

133

compound. They tied people up and beat some French guys who were living upstairs and working for Doctors Without Borders. They tied up and beat everyone in the compound. The thieves were robbing the place, when Dib drove up in his car, the armed gunmen thought the man who ran away had gone to get some help. So, the robbers fled.

They didn't know that the man who ran away, ran to the police to get help and inform the local police what was happening.But the local police said they would not come or do anything until 7 AM. The police wouldn't come and protect us, because the robbers had machine guns.

All I needed was the Lord to be my protector. Since I was living downstairs, it only makes sense they would have broken in the rooms downstairs first, or at the same time as the upstairs, but they never touched me or where I was living. It was just the Grace of God. God was my refuge and my fortress. I kept on trusting in him.

A few weeks later, a soldier tried to get money from me. As he asked me for money, he put his bayonet a few inches away from my throat. Many times, acting dumb is wisdom. I acted as if I didn't notice the bayonet at my throat. His English was bad, so I kept saying "what are you saying - what do you want - I don't understand you". After about fifteen minutes, he gave up and left me alone. I later befriended him and never had another problem with him.

I had conducted a wedding ceremony for a lady who worked at the U. S. Embassy. I had met the U. S. Ambassador and the ranking U. S. Officials and had eaten dinner with several of them a couple of times. In addition to this, I was invited to the Warden's meetings at the U.S. Embassy.

The U. S. Embassy was expecting the government to fall at any time. The soldiers had not been paid for six months. Soldiers were robbing many people. Eight missionary families had been robbed in several weeks. The U. S. Embassy was preparing us to get ready to evacuate the country. We all knew of the chaos and killing rampage that had gone on in Liberia, the country below us, after the fall of that government. No one wanted it to happen to Sierra Leone.

The value of human life was almost nothing among the soldiers. I was talking to a high-ranking official in the Sierra Leone government. We were discussing possible solutions for the problems of Sierra Leone. This person told me that the war with the rebels of Charles Taylor, that was being fought in Sierra Leone was gradually getting worse and worse.

I suggested that they use financial incentives and pay the soldiers for every prisoner that they captured. I was then told that they tried the incentive plan, but it didn't work. They had told the soldiers that the government of Sierra Leone would pay six dollars for every rebel that they killed.

So, the soldiers began to go into Sierra Leone villages and kill Sierra Leone innocent people. The soldiers would kill innocent people and cut their heads off. They would bring the heads back, so they would get paid six dollars. They had to stop the incentive plan. However, life in Sierra Leone was only worth six dollars to many soldiers.

This same person, that was very high in the government, also told me that earlier in the war the Sierra Leone soldiers, were so peaceful that they did not want to kill the enemy. So, the government gave them some pills that made them want to kill people. The government gave drugs to the soldiers to make them want to kill people, without realizing what would happen because of the drugging of their soldiers.

The atrocities that happened in this war can be traced back to drugging the soldiers to make them want to kill.

My question to this day, which I did not ask, is what government developed and sold drugs to the Sierra Leone government to make people want to kill. Are governments still giving drugs to soldiers to make them kill their enemies?

I began to know of so many abuses of the government, that I became angry in my spirit. Almost everyone, including their own government, was abusing the people of Sierra Leone. I began to pray in tongues, eight to twelve hours a day against the government. I knew God was angry at how the government was abusing the people. I knew the Holy Spirit was supernaturally praying against the government of Sierra Leone.

I then had a dream, or vision about the three spirits or three giant serpents that were controlling, ruling, and reigning in Sierra Leone. There was a giant white serpent, a blue one and a green one. This was also the colors of the flag. They were the spirit of fear – white with fear, the spirit of greed (envy and jealousy) – green with envy and the spirit of idolatry (whoredoms or religious spirits) the blue serpent was the spirit of idolatry or whoredoms. These three spirits were revealed, so I took authority over them with a holy vengeance.

I had been fervently praying, up to 16 hours a day in tongues. For weeks I would wake up praying in tongues by the Holy Spirit. There was anger in my spirit against the government. I felt I was praying for a powerful change in the government. The fourth day of unrelenting praying in tongues, the government was overthrown. I woke up on Thursday morning hearing the gunfire.

The battle to overthrow the government had begun. The soldiers from the war front had taken over the "statehouse" where the President's office was. You could hear the gunfire throughout the capital city of Freetown.

After I got dressed, I had a great joy in my spirit, a great sense of excitement, but also some fear, for I knew the situation could become the killing fields of Africa, if God did not intervene.

The U. S. Embassy/Consulate was downtown across the street from the "statehouse". There was no way to get there, so I decided I had better go to the Cape Sierra Hotel where several American Embassy personnel were living. When I arrived at the hotel, I met Jamie and some others that I knew. We all decided to stay at the hotel until we see what would happen. Since there were many United Nations personnel and World Bank officials staying at the hotel, the hotel would become a U.N. Safe Haven. Before the end of the day, the U.N. Flag would be flying outside the hotel.

I began talking to some Sierra Leone friends and discovered that there was to be a major attack on the statehouse at 1 PM. Since the embassy was across the street, I immediately told Jamie, who gave the information to the US embassy. They did not have the report yet of the planned attack. After the embassy learned of the situation and had confirmation of the planned attack, they had most of the people leave that building for a more secure location.

It wasn't long before they had gunfire and bullets entering the U.S. Counsel offices at the US Embassy. The situation was deteriorating. The government was losing control. Chaos was beginning. The soldiers were stealing cars and robbing businesses. The situation was becoming a free for all. For the next three days, there was a steady stream of gunfire, bombs, explosions, and the rocket's red glare from bombs bursting in air combined with tracers on bullets. It made the sky actually very pretty, almost like being at a firework show.

While all of this was happening.

I began to feel an urgency in my spirit to get to the non-governmental radio station. I felt I had to teach Psalm 91 and have the people of Sierra Leone pray Psalm 91. I felt if I didn't do this, Freetown would become a place of total lawlessness and senseless killing. I told several friends what I felt I needed to do. They thought I was crazy. All the wise counsel was to stay in the U.N. safe haven. I knew wisdom said to stay, my fears said to stay, but was moved in my spirit, beyond my fears to go to the radio station. I decided to find some way to get to the radio station.

I tried to find a taxi to take me to the radio station. No one wanted to risk being killed or losing their taxi to a soldier with a gun. I couldn't really blame them, but I had to go. I had no choice. I must obey God.

Since no one would take me, I started walking to go to the radio station. Finally, one taxi driver had mercy on me. He didn't want to see me walking the streets of Freetown. He was afraid that I, being a white man, might be killed. So, he took me.

We made a very quick trip to the station. He went as fast as he could, he wanted as little risk as possible. We went speeding down the road, about 70mph on a small tiny street, so fast no one would be able to slow us down, shoot us or steal his car.

When we arrived at the Bintumani Hotel, where the station was based, the driver said he would wait for me, unless he saw it was getting dangerous. I jumped out of the car and ran to the studio.

Since I had been buying time on this station, all the guys knew me. I told them what I wanted to do.

The D.J. Who was on the air told me to let him know when I was ready, and he would switch over to me. I had about two minutes to prepare. I found a Bible in the station. I knew if I said anything, taking anyone's side, I would probably be killed. One wrong word would probably mean death.

The D.J. switched it over to me. I began to teach the security and protection that people could enter, if they would pray Psalm 91. I took them through it in 15 minutes I then prayed Psalm 91 over the country. I encouraged the people to continue praying Psalm 91 throughout this conflict. I then left the studio, my mission accomplished.

As I was going to the taxi, the station engineer was running to get some things from his office. Prince George said "thank you so much for coming here and doing what you did. We needed it". I immediately left.

Within five minutes, soldiers came to the station and took over the station. I only had a small window of opportunity to do what I did, but I had obeyed God. I am convinced that because people began to pray Psalm 91, is the reason why only a handful of people were killed in this government takeover. God honors his word. God confirms his word to those who believe it.

I returned to the hotel. The daily rates were about $75 - $100. I had about $60, if I remember right. I thought Lord, only you know how much money I have. If you want me to stay here, you must provide.

The man I was staying with was Dib Shahine. Dib also worked for the hotel. The hotel gave Dib a free room with two beds in it, so Dib offered me free lodging at the hotel. I could stay in his room. Since he would be working, I basically had the room to myself. God had provided again.

The next five days at the hotel was interesting and exciting. The soldiers would continually be coming into the hotel. They would be drinking, and at times be drunk. They would have RPG's or grenade launchers on their back. They would have the machine guns in their hands. They would drive up to the hotel many times in stolen vehicles. We never knew which soldiers were government soldiers and which were the rebel soldiers.

The soldiers were in such fear that sometimes I would

look at them, praying in my mind asking the Lord if he wanted me to go to them and witness to them. I was just interested in their salvation. They were afraid simply from me looking at them.

One soldier told one of the hotel managers to make me stop looking at them.

Here they had all the guns, weapons, and power. Yet, they were afraid of a person who was just a simple preacher. They were afraid of me. I had no guns. I had no power over them. Yet, they recognized that there was something different about me, and they were afraid of it. They were in power. They were in control. They had the guns. Yet, they were afraid of me. All I did was look at them, so I tried to stop looking at them. I didn't want them to flip out and start killing people.

I was at the United Nations briefings. I had the information from the U. S. Government and the British government, but God knows what no one else knows. I was reading a paper from a distance that the UN Ambassador had. There were notes from his private meetings with both sides of the conflict. I happened to be standing behind him as he was updating the people about what was going on.

The General who was telling lies about me, and wanted me killed planned the original coup. He was really the leader of the planned coup.

Captain Valentine Strasser and his men were protesting, merely because they wanted to be paid. They had not been paid in months.

After President Momoh was overthrown, the new leader was this other man, General Talawali. Captain Strassa did not plan the coup, but he became the new head of state. The General that planned the coup was overthrown and replaced with 28-year-old Valentine Strasser.

The soldiers knew the General was corrupt and he was

reportedly told leave the country or die. He chose to leave the country. So, my greatest enemy left the country.

No one really knew who was going to be the new head of state. Most people thought there was only one coup, but there were in fact two different coups.

Captain Strasser had accepted Christ years earlier but was backslidden. Captain Strasser oversaw security for Eric Cowlings Miracle and Healing Crusade. Within a few months after this crusade, he became the head of state.

I personally believe the Holy Spirit anointed him to lead the country during that time. If he had not been president, or head of state, the radio station would not have happened. He was far from a perfect leader, but God had anointed him to do it, and he accomplished what God anointed him to do.

Because there were two government takeovers, the U.S. evacuated all American Citizens. The U. S. Ambassador asked me if I was going to leave. I told him no, I was going to stay. I told him if I left Sierra Leone now, the radio station would never become a reality. He said, well, it is your choice.

The day of the "Americans evacuation", Eric and I talked at the beach. I told him the Lord had given me scriptures showing Freetown would be safe, and I should stay. Eric had the same witness about staying, just as Russ Tatroo felt he should stay. All of us were Americans, but we trusted our God more than the American Embassy or American Intelligence.

A friend of mine worked with the International Rescue Committee, and had U. S. Embassy credentials. So, she asked me to go to the embassy with her and to go to the Red Cross with her. I immediately said yes. It was fun to be going through Freetown in a vehicle marked "International Rescue Committee".

For me, life was intended to be exciting. When I get bored, the Lord usually gives me something fun and exciting to do. Jamie evacuated with the other Americans, and she couldn't understand why I wanted to stay, when I knew more about what had gone on than most of the people. She knew I had even read the notes of the U. N. Ambassador from his meetings with the new government officers. I knew their doubts and their problems, but I knew my God.

Some World Bank officials told me that they could almost guarantee that if I stayed, we would get the permits for the radio station. They explained some of the reasons and mentality of the new government. I felt their wisdom was the wisdom of God, and I acted on it.

The following Monday, the new government was trying to be established and be received by the people. At 9 AM, one man who worked closely with the British Government had to go to his office. He asked me if I wanted to go.

I said yes. In fact, I needed to make appointments to speak with some of the new government ministers. So, we ventured into Freetown. I can guarantee there were no traffic problems that Monday morning. It took less than eight minutes to get to his office.

When I called the Permanent Secretary of Information and Broadcasting, he said "Kyle, come on up to the office this morning". As I made my way to the twelve story Youjou Building, it was very intimidating. Soldiers were everywhere. Some were obviously drunk and had little sleep. The weapons, the machine guns, the bullets, RPG's, AK 47's, the grenade launchers, they were everywhere.

When I walked into the office of the Permanent Secretary of Information and Broadcasting, I was greeted very enthusiastically. The Director of Sierra Leone Broadcasting Service immediately began to say, "I don't want you to think that because I am a Moslem is the reason I have been blocking the radio station all this time".

For the first time, I was learning who was blocking the radio station and working against it. That day I visited many government offices. Soldiers were everywhere. Intimidation like I had never seen. But the doors were open like they had never been before. I began to have help like I had never experienced before.

Within a few weeks, much progress was made. New applications were made to the new government. I left Sierra Leone with Mrs. Angela Gooding, having all our paperwork and promising to help follow up on the station.

This trip, many had received Christ. Many received healing. Many things had happened. It was obvious God was with me. I was in his perfect will.

When I left Africa, I had to return through Paris, so I wrote Celia and she told me to stay at her apartment and that she would be in Germany with the Demonts. I arrived in Paris and made my way to Rambuillet, which is where Celia's apartment was. It was so nice to be back in civilization. Electricity, hot water, peace, all those things I took for granted. I could even watch television. What a miracle!

For a week, I stayed by myself. I just prayed, read, studied and rested. I discovered how stressful my life had been, when I was watching a funny movie. Suddenly, I wanted to start crying for no reason. I realized I had enough rest, at peace enough, that emotionally, the release I needed took place.

I had been literally at the point of being killed many times. There was constant shooting. There was stress of so many different kinds. It was exciting. It was adventuresome, but it had a price.

I was beginning to learn I needed emotional support, just as I needed the prayer support and the financial support.

Many ministries fail because the minister does not receive the emotional support that they need. Financial support is required because it takes money to do anything. Spiritual and prayer support are very necessary because you cannot win spiritual battles without the prayer and spiritual support. But I was just beginning to realize even if you were a person of great faith, accomplishing impossible things, you still needed the emotional support from other people.

With all the things I had gone through, such as being shot at by soldiers, preachers lying to me, the continued financial stress, the political stress, many receiving Christ, many being healed, and yet it seemed at times, the Lord was the only one who cared about a lost, dying world. Where were the people I needed to stand with me? Where were the people to hold up my hands as they held up Moses' hands? Where were they?

CHAPTER XVIII

GOVERNMENT APPROVAL THE TIME TO BEGIN

In the new government, the husband of Angela Gooding, Mr. Arnold Gooding, became our equivalent of Attorney General, and a cabinet member. So, when it finally came time for our paperwork to be presented to the cabinet, he had to get involved.

The Ministry of Information and Broadcasting lost our paperwork. So, Mr. Gooding had to send someone from the Justice Department to find our paperwork, so it could be presented to the cabinet.

In October of 1992, in a cabinet meeting, the Sierra Leone Government approved the permit for Grace International to be able to broadcast worldwide without restrictions on power. I was sent a copy of the cabinet approval in the U.S.A. I rejoiced, for what God had promised, he had performed.

I will always be grateful to the Valentine Strassa government that granted us the permission for the radio station. It had taken about three years to gain the preliminary approval and finally the approval of cabinet. The Lord used the Goodings to help bring to pass his will and his plan. They were one of the few who were helping without a selfish motive, only a desire to help the country, and help promote the Gospel of Christ. God had to do many things to get the people in power that would approve his plan. Through faith and patience, we had obtained the promise. Now we must begin.

I kept having dreams of the suffering black people calling for me to come and help. I was doing all I could do. I didn't know how God was going to do it, but I knew he would provide.

By December, God had provided the money for me to go to Sierra Leone. When I arrived in Sierra Leone, I had little money and I must establish a radio station. I had never even worked at a radio station, yet the Lord had told me to start a radio station. I was ready to step out in faith and see what God was going to do.

The first thing that was necessary was to begin to select a staff. But the staff would be unique, because we didn't have money to pay them. It would be a staff of people who were called of God, called to radio and willing to live by faith. Many people wanted to work for us until they found out they would have to work and learn with no pay. Now I see this caused us to get a core of people who were more committed than most ministries ever see.

One of the first people that started working on staff was Rev. Kromah. He was about 60 years old, a Baptist, and had vision for starting a radio station in Sierra Leone. He brought a pastoral gift and wisdom that the staff was in dire need of. He also brought public relations experience that we needed. (Later I was told he was a plant from the government to watch us)

We realized that we needed to start a six weeks broadcast school, so God really began to bring in people with broadcasting experience who volunteered to teach in our little broadcasting school.

We would have about 60 students and eventually about 30 people would be on the staff from this group. I will always be grateful to those who volunteered.

Since most of the people who worked for us were young, the disciplinarian was Winston Togbah, he was from Freetown Bible Training Center.

Mrs. Hannah Dixon became the secretary and treasurer, but more than that she became the station mother. Most on the staff called her Mama D. She was a mature woman who had a motherly gift.

Rev. Kromah, Mama D., and Winston would basically be managing the station when I was not there. Rev. Kromah and Mrs. Dixon were Sierra Leoneans and Winston was a Liberian.

Our goal from the beginning was to have a station staffed with nationals. Eventually, Winston would go to Liberia and get the permits to start a station there. This was the core of our staff, in addition, of course to me. During the process of setting up the station and selecting a site for our office, an unusual event took place.

I had a dream that showed me that the government was going to fall apart if they didn't stop and fix some things.

Well, one day Femi Antony stopped at the guest house and we began to talk about the dreams we had. Femi worked in the government and had helped me on several occasions. We sometimes disagreed doctrinally but we usually had some good Christian fellowship. We both felt the government needed to declare a week of repentance, fasting and prayer.

I believe at about the same time, other friends of Mrs. Gooding were also sensing that the government needed a time of fasting and prayer, as well.

Through the efforts of many people, Captain Valentine Strasser, head of State of Sierra Leone, issued a decree. There was to be a week of fasting, prayer, and repentance. No one was to be selling alcohol, the clubs were to be closed. Moslems and Christians alike were asked to join in a time of fasting, prayer and repentance.

I had never seen such a change that took place. The youth began competing in different sectors of the city, to see who could do the best beautification project. Curbs were painted. Streets were cleaned. The attitudes of people began to change. A unity was being developed.

On the last day of the fast, I had two people around me, say that they were interested in becoming a Christian. I prayed with them to receive Christ. I was concentrating on getting the station started, not getting people saved, but spiritually, there were changes taking place because of the week of fasting and prayer. It became so easy to lead people to Christ.

For months people were talking about the changes that began at the week of prayer, fasting, and repentance. The changes were so obvious that Moslem, Christian, and even non-Christian saw it.

What very few people realized was that at about this time, during this week, the government uncovered five plots to overthrow the government. If they had not had the week of prayer, fasting and repentance, they would have been overthrown and the government would have fallen apart.

The first station that we planned was to be an FM station, so our frequency assignment was 93.0 MHZ. FM.

Many people were jealous. The Baptist, Methodist and others had tried to get permits for a Christian radio station for over 30 years. Most of the other denominations had tried also, as had the Council of Churches of Sierra Leone. They couldn't understand how we got the permits. Many said we paid bribes. Many said many things. To me it was just the Grace of God. God said to do it, and I obeyed.

The rumors began to spread about me and the staff. Certain religious people did not want a Christian radio station, and many sure didn't want a Christian radio station that believed in miracles, and that the gifts of the Holy Spirit were for today.

The school of broadcasting was getting planned. Plans of getting the churches involved were developed. We had a frequency assignment. I needed to return to the U.S. and get the equipment for the first Christian radio station in Sierra Leone. God was working. It was finally becoming a reality.

The broadcasting school was going to start in a couple of weeks. Allen who worked with the Institute for Sierra Leone Languages was our main teacher of practical broadcasting. Felix George, the acting director of S.L.B.S. would volunteer to teach, as did several others. The school was in good hands.

We had an office. We had the beginnings of a great staff.

When I left, I had almost no money.

This time I had to return through Washington, D. C. There were some scheduling changes, so I missed my connecting flight in Washington, D. C. I didn't have $40.00 for a motel room, so I slept in a chair at the airport. This didn't bother me, for God was working to bring the radio station to pass at last.

In the middle of the night when I was sleeping, I heard a voice. It said, "I am with you to help you". I awoke and saw there was no one around. I knew God was trying to reassure me that he was going to help me.

CHAPTER XIX

FM.93 IS ON THE AIR!!

I really thought that when I finally got the permits, people would be ready to help. They would finally see it was God and begin to help financially. I thought people would be eager to help the suffering people of Sierra Leone. I thought that the sincere Christians would want to help. After all, by the grace of God, we had been able to accomplish what denominations had tried to do and could not.

I sent out letters asking for help. I talked to many people. I shared a little in some churches. But people weren't giving. Didn't they understand that this was a great miracle and that we couldn't pass up this opportunity? A Christian radio station, preaching the full gospel in Moslem West Africa - Why couldn't they get the vision? Where was the desire to help a lost, hurting dying world? Couldn't they see we could broadcast to all of Africa and Europe? Millions of people could be saved. What an opportunity!

Some people were quite honest. They said, "we would help if it was any place but Africa, after all, you know how the blacks are". I knew their culture. I knew their sin. This is what made it even more imperative to reach out and help

150

them. They needed the gospel more than anyone.

We all know the stories of Elijah and the widow. God sent Elijah to a woman who had nothing, and through her he would work the miracle of provision, he needed. There would be four people who would make great sacrifices to enable me to take the equipment to Africa. The miracle would happen not through churches or large organizations, but by a handful of people doing what they could, giving beyond their ability.

I had met Dr. Robert Kellum through Forrest McMillan. Dr. Kellum was approaching 70. He was part of the "Friends" denomination and had started the first Christian radio station in the Central African Republic of Burundi. At five years of age, he had a vision of people going to hell. For over 60 years he had been reaching out to the hurting, lost, dying world. He had also worked for Pat Robertson of the 700 Club, as a consultant, as well as Far East Broadcasting Corporation. He was now a retired missionary being on a very fixed income.

Dr. Keller took me under his wing. He gave me a crash course in broadcasting, engineering, and African radio. He started talking to people, trying to get some equipment for the station. One ham radio operator made a home-made copper pipe antenna about five feet long. A Christian radio station in Houston gave him an old exciter which Dr. Keller tried to repair. Dr. Keller ended up giving us his own personal tape deck and a little mixer. But we still needed an FM amplifier.

I found an FM amplifier for about $1200. It was only 100 watts, but it would be a starting point. The problem was, we didn't have the $1200.

My mother, Teddy Hunt, had applied for social security. She had been approved and the government sent her $1,500, which was for several months of back pay. My mother said she felt she was to give the money to buy the RF Amplifier from her check.

Reluctantly, I said yes. I knew it had to be God. The two people who paid for the equipment, or got the equipment, was two people on social security.

It wasn't the rich, God was using to help. It was those who had very little. As Dr. Kellum gave me some of his favorite recording equipment, he almost wept. He did weep later. He knew the equipment we had was so inadequate, but he knew it was a starting point. He knew thousands would commit their life to Christ because of his personal sacrifice, as well as the sacrifice of my mother.

We packed everything in five boxes at the house of Dr. Kellum, in Friendswood, Texas. I would leave from the Houston Airport on Air France.

Bruce Tyler, or Dr. Elder, had paid for my ticket.

As we loaded the car to go to the airport, Dr. Kellum wept, cried, and laughed. He wept because of the souls that would be saved, but he laughed at the equipment we would be using to start the first Christian radio station in Sierra Leone.

As we left Dr. Kellum's house, we prayed that God would work a miracle, because I only had about $300. We had a lot of extra boxes, some were quite heavy. The extra baggage charges should have been about $300 or more.

When I arrived at the airport, I was quite early. Since there was only a handful of people on the flight to Paris, Air France let me check all the boxes and luggage all the way to Freetown. I didn't have to pay anything extra. Praise God! It was truly a miracle.

I arrived in Freetown with a radio station in five boxes. We made it through the airport with no problem. That night I would have the equipment at the guest house. The next morning, we would take the equipment to our office on Pademba Road. The staff was excited to see me and the equipment. Since no one on staff knew much about radio, everyone was pleased with the equipment we had to start with. We all knew it was the starting point.

We found a building that was rarely used by a denomination on Leceister Peak. We had verbal agreements that we would repair the building in exchange for rent. The building was in terrible shape. Six months later, they would change their mind and tell us to leave.

Rev. Kromah and myself had been told several times that this non-full gospel denomination had agreed to our being there. Since they would later say that we had to give them a percentage of the station or move, we left. I had told them we would give them a percentage of the station on the condition that any money received for the station would go to the station. They refused. Obviously, they wanted to use the station to raise money for themselves, and not to help the station. But this is where we started.

The transmitter site was located very high in the mountains around Freetown. We set up the broadcasting microphones by the window. This way, you could see most of Freetown from the studio window. Our studio was on the second floor of the building. As we played music or preached, we could see the hundreds of thousands of people we were reaching.

We didn't have a tower, so some of the guys made a pole out of pieces of trees and put the antenna on top of the house. We didn't have racks for the equipment, so everything was spread out on tables.

After we blew out one or two power transformers, we were finally on the air in April, 1993. It took three and one half years to start what God said to do.

FM.93 is on the air! Tell your friends we will be on the air every night! The first Christian radio station in Sierra Leone is on the air! Now, let's go to some music.

English is the official language in Sierra Leone, but there

are about 12 languages spoken in Sierra Leone. So, we had several people greet the radio audience in the different languages.

My routine for the next several months would be to wake up at 7 AM, pray and prepare for a Bible study in the office at 9 AM. 10 AM till 4 PM I would be involved in administrative duties. At 4 PM we would take a taxi up to the mountains where we would start broadcasting about 5 PM. At 9 PM I would preach until about 10 - 10:30 PM. We would take a taxi back down to Freetown about 10:30. I would arrive at the guest house and eat dinner at 11 PM. I would then go to bed.

On Sundays, I would have an easy day and only work about 9 hours. This would be my normal manner of living until I would leave Sierra Leone. I would average between 80 - 90 hours per week, working for the ministry, receiving no pay, but rejoicing in the privilege of starting the first Christian radio station in the country.

We began hearing reports of the Moslems listening to the station. The Moslem preachers would at times even quote things we said on the radio station. The areas of Freetown that had lots of drug addicts were listening to the station. From the upper class to the lower class, it seemed everyone was listening or knew about the station.

One man who worked for the station was waiting for a taxi or bus. The other man said, "have you listened to that new reggae station, they have some great music".

People loved the contemporary Christian music. We played tapes of Maranatha Praise, Hosanna Praise Tapes, Carmen Tapes, and other contemporary Christian music artists. The people had never heard Christian music that had such life.

The drug addicts, the Moslems, the Christians were all listening. When the government station saw the response, they began to play the Christian music as well. We knew our audience was primarily non-Christian, so we would give altar calls and pray for people to receive Christ several times a night. We were bold, we were evangelistic, we believed in miracles. We were beginning to impact a nation.

One night as I was preaching, a flying snake began to crawl into the window of the studio. In Sierra Leone, there are poisonous snakes that jump through the air 20 to 30 feet. So, this flying snake started crawling in. The studio desk and microphones were directly in front of the windows and the snake. I continued preaching, and as I saw the snake, his entire body about 3 feet long, he moved slowly and wrapped around the window casing. I said something about a snake had just climbed into the windows of the studio.

The other guys with me were outside the studio. The door to the studio was locked from the inside.

The snake was about 3 feet in front of me. His head was about one foot higher than my head. I saw the snake move his head back. I knew he was getting ready to strike. I knew he was planning to attack his prey, me. The instant he drew his head back, knowing he was going to attack, I said "in the name of Jesus Christ - Go". As I said this, the snake fell out of the window. Praise God for the power in Jesus' name.

The devil didn't like people getting saved. He apparently sent a snake to attack me in the second story window. I had never dreamed a snake could enter a window of a two-story building. This was Africa.

This was raw evangelism where the raw, unpolished power of God needed to be displayed. We were not polished professionals, we were just simple people trying to obey God. We were just trying to preach the gospel.

A friend of mine who worked with Eric Cowley wanted to come up and see the station. He had some radio experience from England. He knew what radio stations were supposed to look like.

I said- "if you come, you have to promise not to laugh around the staff".

He said okay. He understood we were just starting. When he arrived at the transmitter site, he saw the antenna and the tower. He couldn't keep from laughing. After he saw our equipment, he really knew it was a miracle that we sounded as good as we did. He really tried to keep from laughing, but he couldn't.

Every night we would have to pass checkpoints that would have soldiers manning them. They would have their machine guns and weapons on them as they searched the vehicle. Many times, they were drunk or on drugs.

One night you could see that they were drunk. They were being very obstinate. One soldier had his pistol in his hand. His finger was on the trigger, the barrel a couple of inches from my head. We all were probably praying under our breath.

Finally, they let us go. If we said anything they didn't like, we would have been in Heaven. Situations like this were quite common. Just the cost of doing business for the Lord in West Africa.

After we had been on the air, I thought I would make a 3-minute offering tape. I read several scriptures and told the needs of the station. I thought the Lord would use this to help supply our financial needs. We would play the 3-minute tape once or twice a day. Within one week, I had messages from three different people in the top of the government telling me to stop trying to get people to give over the radio.

Now, I was really in a dilemma. How could the station survive if we couldn't take up offerings? We had people, including myself, going to all the churches trying to get them to buy radio time. Almost no one wanted time. They thought we should pay them, for them to have a program. We had the lowest price for radio time in the world, and almost no one wanted to buy programs. How could the station survive if we couldn't sell radio time?

We were planning our grand opening on Pentecost Sunday. Everything was planned. The financial pressures were mounting.

I told the staff that realistically, the only thing to do was for me to return to the U.S. to try to raise money. They were trained. They could do the job as well as me. Most on staff agreed. Those that knew everything, knew I needed to return to the U. S. and try to get programming funds.

Before I left I told Ransford Wright I knew he would eventually become the station manager. I never once dreamed that he would be the station manager before I returned. I left to try to raise money and sell radio time.

After I left Sierra Leone, reportedly about 2000 people came for our opening at the City Hall Auditorium. There was enough money raised to keep the station going. Every month would be a miracle. All the staff would be going months at a time without any money. This would be a station built by the sacrifices of those that had nothing, or almost nothing. The spirit of sacrifice was in the staff and in me. We would go years without a salary. A great sacrifice, but souls were getting saved.

CHAPTER XX

LOOKING FOR HELP

To my surprise, amazement, and shame, no one accepted our offer for free radio time. We had offered free radio time to all the major ministries in the US.

After I went to Lakewood Church and personally talked to Brother John Osteen, with Lakewood Church, he said he would send tapes to the station. He was the only major ministry that accepted our offer. We knew the people needed teaching, yet the ministries that were excellent teaching ministries would not accept our free time.

Disappointed, disillusioned, and partially bitter, I became more and more frustrated. No one wanted to help. Brother Osteen was the only one. We decided God must have some other plan. So, we stopped offering free radio time. Some ministries were very skeptical of our free offer, thinking we had some ulterior motive in giving the time. We really had to pray to walk in love and forgiveness.

I had a dream that I was fishing in a river. I caught a huge fish. The fish was so big that it pulled me into the river. I couldn't stop the fish, it was pulling me into the water, yet I had no power to stop it. I had a huge fish on my line, but it was not possible for me to stop the fish or catch it. I wouldn't let go. I was at the point of drowning, but I wouldn't let it go.

I knew the dream was about the radio station. There was a great catch of souls, but the harvest of souls was too big for me to be able to handle. I needed help. I couldn't do it alone. I was at the point of drowning, but I wouldn't give up on the station. The souls were too important. If necessary, I would die to save the souls that would be reached through the station. I couldn't quit. I would put everything into helping the station.

I realized more than ever that I needed help. To me it wasn't important who did the station, if it was done. It was needed. It was in Muslim West Africa.

Several people told me about a certain religious broadcasting network that had said on television that if anyone would get the permits for a radio station or television station out of the U.S., they would help. I had heard the head of this organization say this as well. I wrote to him saying we had the permits and some very limited equipment for radio and could get the permits for television. I reminded him in the letter of what he said. When he responded to my letter, he said they couldn't do it. A year later, he signed an agreement to do a television station with another group in Sierra Leone.

Everyone began to say I didn't want to work with anyone else. After all the religious Broadcasting Network agreed to bring a television station to Sierra Leone. They said I was full of pride and didn't want to ask for help. I knew I could show my letters and the Broadcasting Network's letter. I could prove I was right, but it would only cause more bad publicity for Christian ministries.

I knew one person wanted to sue the broadcasting network and make them do what they said they would do. There had been enough scandals with television preachers. I didn't want anymore. The scandals hurt all the Body of Christ. I figured it was better to have few people think I was a liar, than to have millions of people know another preacher of the gospel was a liar.

There was another television and radio network that had a representative at times in Sierra Leone. We had talked. I told him we would gladly accept any kind of help they would be willing to offer. We could even trade time on our radio station for one of their small stations. It would at least give us exposure in the U. S.

This man told others in Sierra Leone that I didn't want help. I told our staff in a letter to feel free to make him a member of the board, but as usual, it was just another excuse.

I would send letters to all the Charismatic broadcasting ministries that I knew of. I would offer to work with them in any way that they wanted. I just wanted to see the station see its potential. I was ready to give the station to any full gospel broadcasting network that would fully develop the station. No one was interested.

The Lord spoke - "THE STATION NEEDS PRAYER". I thought, Lord, I know that. I then began to ask everyone I knew to pray for the station. Prayer was the thing needed most. If people would pray, everything else would happen.

CHAPTER XXI

GIVING BEYOND MY ABILITY!

I had placed an ad in the Radio World Newspaper for used equipment to help the station in Africa. One radio station in Carlsbad, New Mexico called and said if we came to Carlsbad, we could have some of their old equipment.

So, Bruce Tyler and I went to Carlsbad, with his trailer to get the equipment. Most people in radio would say it wasn't worth much, but God was providing. We were rejoicing in what God was doing. There were reel to reel decks, a couple of old mixers, racks and automation equipment.

I knew people needed to see serious looking equipment. When people saw our studio, they would say we weren't serious. With this equipment, they could never again say we weren't serious. It was very complicated looking equipment. It would help make our station really look professional.

I had been gone for over a year. We needed a new transmitter. We needed cassette decks, CD players, tapes, sound mixers, desks, microphones. We needed so much. How could it be purchased?

I had started building a 2700 square foot house with 5 bedrooms and 3 bathrooms when Veronica and I planned to get married. My grandmother had given me an acre of land. I had built the house starting with $10 in my pocket. But after Veronica decided we would not get married, I lost my motivation to finish the house.

I gave it to my home church for them to use. They didn't do anything with it. So, I basically got the house back. This time I decided to sell it and put all the money into the radio station in Africa.

I decided the only way I could help the station quickly was to sell my house. Ransford Wright had become the station manager. We were now broadcasting from our office on Pademba Road. It wasn't a good location to broadcast from. The staff was getting disillusioned. I had to show the staff I also was making great sacrifices. So, I sold my house and put the proceeds into the station.

It was so much fun. For the first time, we could buy so many things that were needed. The wish list that became a reality included a new transmitter, a generator, a new tower, coax, 12 channel sound mixer, 24 disk CD player, tapes and CD's, cassette decks, microphones, computer, plywood to make custom studio desks, tools and other equipment.

Dr. Terry Elder bought a used Volkswagen station wagon. Bruce Tyler volunteered to pay for a container to send all the equipment to Africa. We were finally going to have a vehicle. God was working. We were also sending lots and lots of used clothes.

Bruce and I drove all the clothes and equipment down to Houston. The Volkswagen was also in Houston. Dr. Kellum also had some other donations and advice.

We loaded the container. The container would take over 2 months to arrive in Sierra Leone, West Africa.

Chapter XXII

AFRICA BY WAY OF CHILE

The Lord had also spoken and told me to go to Chile. So, the day after we sent the container to Africa, I left to go to South America.

The Lord had told me I would get married in Chile. I was very curious to see what would happen. I stayed with Mariano and Angelica Arancibia, the friends and the family I had stayed with years earlier. It was so nice to be back in an atmosphere of love, acceptance, and where people believed in me. The Lord sent me with a message, but he also had another thing in mind.

As I was returning from Pastor Rafael Martinez' house, I was in the metro, or subway. The Lord said "get off at this metro station and you will meet Veronica. This is a sign unto you that you are to marry Veronica".

God was true to his word. As I got out of the metro train, I walked up the steps and there was Veronica. After several other signs and confirmations, Veronica and I were married December 10, 1994.

Two days after we returned from our honeymoon, I had to return to the U. S., so I could go to Africa. Veronica had told her boss that she would work until the end of January, and train someone to take her place. So, two weeks after we were married, I was off to Africa.

When Veronica found out I had sold "our" house and put all the money into the ministry, she was angry, frustrated, cried, and yet understood. She said, "We will never be able to have a house like that, it was built with your love for me".

I had to remind her that she was the one that canceled our wedding plans a couple of years earlier, not me. Giving up the house is still a point of contention. I know to never bring the subject up, especially since we didn't have a house of our own. But I know the Lord will reward us for the sacrifice of our house, so that souls would be saved. We will eventually have a house better than the one we put into the ministry. I know the Lord is faithful.

The Lord sometimes works in very unusual ways. Sometimes we can't understand why some things happen, until afterward.

Veronica had to get a visa from the Sierra Leone government. Since there wasn't an embassy in Chile, I had to get a landing visa in Sierra Leone and send it to her and meet her with the original at the airport. After about 100 meetings, we finally received her visa to come to Sierra Leone. This was the end of February.

Veronica was, of course, furious because it was taking so long, after all we had only been together for two weeks before I had to leave Chile. Then for the next 3 months Veronica had so much trouble in getting the ticket to go to Sierra Leone, that it was unreal. The money went from Texas, to California, to Chile, to Puerto Rica, to Iceland, to Chile, to Texas, to London, before she had tickets that would be used to come to Sierra Leone. The delays were literally unbelievable.

She first bought a ticket to go standby. After about one

month, she had not been able to go. Finally, in May, she was to arrive in Freetown. There were many things that God apparently knew that I wouldn't have done if my wife had been with me.

Many times, I would be working 16 hours a day. Usually I would have to leave and be in the office at 9 AM and would go to bed at about 1 or 2 AM. If Veronica had been with me, I would not have been able to put the time that needed to be put into the station. I am sure this is part of the reason for the delays.

Veronica was quite frustrated with me when she finally arrived. We were physically separated for five months after our honeymoon, so you know Veronica is a different type of woman to be able to put up with a very different lifestyle. She went from a life of security and predictability, to a life of insecurity and unpredictability.

When I arrived in Sierra Leone, the container had already arrived, but because of the bureaucratic nightmare, we couldn't get the container out of port. Eventually, Captain Valentine Strasser, the Head of State, would personally have to get involved before we could get the container. Two months after the container arrived, we finally could receive all the equipment we had sent.

The U. S. Ambassador had been working to get all the Americans and American missionaries to leave Sierra Leone.

The civil war was getting worse. Many times, you could hear the bombs dropping. The stories of the war were awful. People were being burned to death, trapped in buses. Pregnant women were having their bellies cut open with machetes to see if they had a boy or a girl. Thousands of people were being killed. Catholic nuns were kidnaped and reportedly sexually abused. European workers were also being kidnaped by the rebel faction.

Twice while I was in Freetown, I could feel the ground shake because of the explosion of bombs. At one time the fighting was within 20 miles of Freetown. The rebels would take young people from one village, drug them and put them on the front lines as they would attack the next village. Raping women, robberies, lawlessness and chaos were prevailing in the provinces of the country.

The U. S. Ambassador had told me and others who attended the warden's meetings, that she would write a letter to our organizations telling how good a job we were doing, but that they recommended strongly that we leave the country. The Ambassador was doing everything in her power to get us to leave. Yet, some of us stayed.

One small denomination was ordered to leave by their denomination. This was a blessing, because we could rent their mission house and use it. We could have the house and transmitter site at one location. This would be where we would move the radio station to. This would be where I planned to live with my new wife.

I went to look at one place for a transmitter site. It was in a village around Leciester Peak. As I was returning from looking at the house, we had to go through a military check point.

As we were stopped and being searched, I saw a woman sergeant telling another soldier, "I want you to get me his wedding ring". She was at a distance, but I could hear her quite clearly. We left as quickly as possible, before the other man could get to us.

It was almost miraculous I could hear them talking. I decided not to return to that place because I didn't want to be robbed of my wedding ring. Things like this were a common occurrence during these times of civil war.

Another time the police were going to arrest me for some

outrageous claim. They wanted me to give them a bribe. I refused, so they planned to arrest me and take me to court. After going through a lot of harassment, they decided to let me go. If I had not been the owner and manager of a radio station, I am sure they would have arrested me.

They only let me go after I told them that several cabinet ministers had wanted us to do real news stories, I said we did not want to do that, because we wanted to be neutral, for the gospel was our mission. But if we did decide to start doing real news, the first thing we would do would be about corruption in the police department. They then let me go.

I had remodeled the house in Freetown in preparation for my wife to be joining me. It had new floor covering, paint, cabinets, etc. It was a nice compound, clean, and even had a generator.

Yet, at times, despite efforts of cleanliness, there were scorpions, spiders, and other bugs entering the house. One day I even found a large rat in the toilet. Another time I found a snake in the kitchen and killed it. Another time a snake was by the car and we killed it.

By Sierra Leone standards, we were living in luxury. We had electricity, a washer, dryer, and even a microwave oven. Yet, there were these typical African distractions. No big deal for a country boy like me, but my wife was a city girl.

A time of war is a time that is exceedingly dangerous, but a time that can be more fruitful for Christ's sake than any other time. I told Veronica "thank you for giving me the opportunity to have this war time ministry experience".

Dr. Robert Smith, a friend and the President of the Red Sea Mission, was living with me. He would usually teach 3 days a week. I would preach 6 days a week.

We had also given some time to five churches in Freetown, who would also be preaching once a night. The rest of the time would be music. On my radio program, I would really try to let the Holy Spirit do what he wanted to do. Sometimes it would be teaching. Sometimes it would be the Gifts of the Spirit. Sometimes it would be praise and sometimes even laughter by the Holy Spirit.

We had reports of many people being saved, healed, receiving the baptism of the Holy Spirit, fire or heat coming upon people as I prayed for them, and even people laughing hilariously by the inspiration of the Holy Spirit.

I was told that many times at Fourah Bay College, that people would start running to their radios when I would come on the air. I would try to always make myself available to the gifts of the Holy Spirit. It was because of the gifts of the Spirit that many people would experience the supernatural, and as a result, be wanting to listen to my program.

One night I knew beyond a shadow of a doubt, that some rebels were listening to the station. I knew from Embassy reports that they were planning an attack. I knew from other sources that one man was planning a government overthrow. I knew these people were listening.

Then I said by inspiration of the Holy Spirit, "There are some people planning to do something; you know what it is. If you do it, you will be killed. If you do what you are planning, you will be killed". I knew in my mind, but also in my spirit, who it was.

After the program, I talked to another man. He had the same witness in his spirit about what I said. We both felt that it literally stopped a planned attack. We will only know the truth when we get to heaven, but many felt the same thing. Being led by the Holy Spirit many of us believed, stopped at attack on the capital city.

Another weekend, the U. S. Embassy had all the Americans ready for an attack. Everyone seemed to be convinced it was coming. They were expecting it for several weeks.

One night I had a planned message, but the Holy Spirit came on me in a special way. I preached a message about fear, and that in Christ there was no fear. I then challenged everyone to commit to going to their family, friends, and neighbors and pray with them to receive Christ, IF, IF, IF they began to hear bombs.

Bombs and gunfire create fear. Jesus Christ and being ready for heaven is the answer to the fear of death. It was a message inspired by the Holy Spirit. Many people were convinced that the message created fear in the devil. The devil knew if there was a military attack, the Christians were going to start witnessing. The stations would go into an evangelistic drive like no one had ever seen. We almost wanted the attack to come, because we knew hundreds of thousands of people would be praying to receive Christ.

The attack didn't happen, many of us are convinced that it was because the devil was afraid of losing thousands of people out of his kingdom to the Kingdom of Christ. This is what ministry was intended to be; effective, exciting, and eternal.

Well, the devil tried to attack the station from several angles. He was determined to stop it. We would eventually overcome, but he looked for the weakest points to hit you.

There was first an attack on me, by several denominations. People were saying that I was on drugs, that I was in adultery, that I was only interested in money and lots of other lies. It got so bad that once a week we would have rumor control at the office. We would try to find out what the latest bad rumors were, about me or the staff. Even the head of a multi-denominational evangelical group said, "no one sells their house and puts the money into the ministry, unless they have a hidden agenda". I was being attacked not by the world, but by the religious people.

The attacks got so bad that the denomination we had leased the building from tried to tell us to leave the building. Since we wouldn't leave, we had a year's contract paid in full, the generator was sabotaged, and the water supply was sabotaged. I eventually had to write a letter to the president of the denomination, telling him about the attempted breach of a written contract, slander, and a whole list of immoral or illegal activities that I had seen or been told about in their denomination in Sierra Leone. Reluctantly, they let us continue in their mission house until the end of the contract.

One of the weakest links was to be my wife. She was born and raised in Santiago, Chile. One Chilean friend of mine said she, Veronica, wasn't like her, but was a Chilean Fina, or culturally higher than she was. Santiago is a prosperous, educated city that has few blacks and is much cleaner than most South American cities. Veronica was an educated city girl, she had seen videos of Sierra Leone, but she was far from being prepared for it.

Before Veronica arrived in Sierra Leone, she was told about the black men raping white women, the Nuns. (Except occasionally during the war, very few white women were ever raped in Sierra Leone.)

Veronica knew about the war. She knew about the poverty. She knew about some of the problems. Mentally she knew. She thought she was prepared, but then she finally came.

I met Veronica at the airport. I had the head of security meet her on the tarmac to help her bypass the line. He was going to her at my request to help her.

All Veronica knew, was this giant black guy, a soldier with dangerous looking guns and bullets draped over his body, was meeting her and say come with me. She did not know I sent him. The head of the Airport Security was helping me and her, because I had a letter from a friend of the President.

I met her and helped her go through customs. I had gotten special permission to meet her, before she went through customs. We went through the airport with very few problems.

Veronica was terrified.

I could see the dirt, the filth, the smell, the lack of etiquette was getting to her. We put the bags in the car. We started to go toward the ferry on our way back to the capitol city, Freetown.

We then had to stop at a military check point; lots of soldiers were around, big, black, and bold. They weren't very polite. But nothing out of the ordinary. The soldiers at this check point were in the middle of nowhere. One soldier then decided to look in her suitcases. They took the bags out and they went through her underwear and other clothes. We put the suitcases back in the car and left.

Veronica began to have a complete emotional breakdown. She began to cry uncontrollably for the next 3 hours. The more she saw, the worse she became. She wasn't prepared for the filth, the rudeness, the lack of culture, the people, the poverty, the living conditions. How could I love her and want her to come here to this place, she asked?

There were so many people in Freetown because of the war, that the streets were jammed with people. Veronica would almost lose complete emotional control, every time we started to go into Freetown. Culture shock unlike I had never dreamed or even thought of.

By the end of the first week, Veronica could go into the center of Freetown. For the first 20 days, she would demand to return to Chile.

I began to be afraid that if just part of the things the U.S. Embassy said would happen, did happen, Veronica might lose all emotional control and have a complete nervous breakdown. Eventually I reluctantly said, I think you should return to Chile.

I was still trying to decide if she should return to Chile, when Veronica and I were driving to the airlines office. A policeman tried to get me to stop. I knew he just wanted a bribe. I knew if I stopped there would be lots of hassle.

I then knew that Veronica would freak out with being arrested in Africa as part of a shakedown for money. I knew she wasn't mentally or emotionally prepared for ministry in a literal war zone. I loved her too much to let her stay.

So, after being together for a short time, she would return to Chile. I didn't stop for the policeman, but he convinced me that Veronica, who I loved so much, must leave. I would once again be alone.

The devil didn't stop with just attacking my wife. Three days after she arrived in Freetown, we had a solid-state radio transmitter engineer come and check out our transmitter. It was putting out less than half the rated output power. While he was checking it out, he short circuited it and blew out the major components. Now we couldn't operate. He also blew out our backup transmitter.

Since the parts would be sent, but not the correct, working parts, and the correct parts would have to come from Europe - to the States - to Africa, it would be several months before we could go back on the air with even close to the same power.

The same engineer also short circuited our backup transmitter as well, when we decided to use it. It took about six engineers, but we finally found a good engineer. We finally got our backup transmitter fixed, after the parts were stolen in the mail.

Six weeks after my wife left Sierra Leone, I left. I knew I was leaving the station in good hands. We had an Advisory Board and an Operational Board of Directors. Ransford was the manager, but it was God's radio station.

The station would come back on the air. The backup

transmitter was fixed. Our main transmitter was fixed. I was able to purchase and send a high-gain FM antenna to the station. We were now broadcasting with about 3000 watts E.R.P.

There were many struggles, but God always helped us overcome. In February 1996, we had to leave the mission house. What would happen? We had no money. We had no place. What would the Lord do?

I had no money. I had sold everything and put it into the station. I was in debt on my credit cards. I had put everything into the station. I saw no other option. What could we do? What would the Lord do?

I remembered a dream I had in Sierra Leone. The Lord spoke and said, "many people have financial problems and the lack of money because they don't take authority over the devil, who tries to hinder it from coming in".

I also remembered a dream that had the lady who conducted our civil marriage ceremony in it. In this dream, she was taking authority over the spirit of Antichrist. After she did this in the dream, love began to flow in the church where she was. She was a person in authority over marriages, taking authority over spirits of Antichrist.

I thought maybe I needed to change my doctrine. Maybe I really needed to believe it was really the devil, or spirits of Antichrist that was trying to create the poverty and marriage problems. Could it really be that the station was in the will of God, but it was Satan hindering it, as he hindered the Apostle Paul? Is the problem really the devil, or is it me?

Before I left the U.S. I had become bitter. My heart wasn't right with God. I was mad at the Lord. I tried to quit the ministry, but when you are the head of it, it is almost impossible to quit.

I felt like the Lord had told me to start a station in the

South of Chile. But I no longer had the spiritual strength to fight. I felt weak. I could no longer do it alone. I needed help.

Pastor Rafael Martinez asked me to minister when I arrived in Chile, and I told him I couldn't. I said my heart isn't right. I have bitterness and need to be healed before I preach. I am sorry.

The station would go on with a bright future in the hands of God and the staff. The US Embassy even worked with the station to provide a tower space for the station since we had been playing Voice of America news every day on the station. It is now covering the entire country under the direction of Ransford.

CHAPTER XXIII

A LETTER FROM GOD

I had been trying to obey God in ministry for almost 17 years. I had seen miracles few people had ever seen. I had seen God do so many wonderful things. Thousands of people had prayed to receive Christ and had received my ministry. I had preached in person or on radio in about 30 countries. Countless people had been healed or received a touch from God. I had seen visions of Jesus, angels, demons, and even judgment day. The Lord had spoken to me countless times, as he had spoken to Samuel. It seemed as if it was an audible voice. I had had more supernatural experiences than anyone I knew. Yet, something was wrong in my ministry.

Out of my frustration, I wrote a letter to several of the more mature people on my mailing list. It was a letter of resignation, resigning from the ministry. If the Lord didn't meet the obligations, I was going to quit the ministry. If people were not going to help, I was quitting. If they received no more letters, it was because I was serious about quitting the ministry. Some people were offended at my letter, thinking it was a manipulation tactic to get them to give. I was serious.

Since people didn't respond with help, I stopped sending

out any newsletters or anything. After all, it took money to send out newsletters. I was serious. I could no longer do the ministry alone. I needed financial, spiritual, and emotional support. Three or four people responded, but I could not continue with the ministry. I was too tired. I was burned out. I couldn't go on. So, I quit from the ministry.

I then returned to Chile to be with my wife. My wife brought a lot of changes into my life. A lot of changes possibly needed to be made, even though they weren't all the changes she thought should be made. Conflicts usually create change.

Sometimes the only way the Lord can get us to change, is to allow us to go through conflicts. One of the major areas of conflict that she had with me was the message of faith and a lot of the charismatic teachings I had been taught and preached. She had been taught about faith and healing, but because she didn't receive her healing, she thought it must be false doctrine.

She didn't understand that a doctrine can be a Bible doctrine, but because it isn't taught properly, it doesn't work. Some important aspects of faith and healing had been left out. Since she heard a message of faith and healing, she thought she understood it. When it didn't work for her, it created a lot of confusion. So, she found a church that believed a basic full gospel message but attacked the message of faith.

Veronica and I loved each other, knew it was God's will for us to be married, yet we had some very strong doctrinal conflicts. After we were married, we just wouldn't discuss doctrinal issues. Her experience and her church taught against many of the things that I knew were true and had lived and experienced. Lots of people couldn't understand our marriage and our relationship. We really loved each other. My love for her was the most important thing, not our being in doctrinal agreement.

Years earlier I was complaining to God about what one minister was teaching. The Lord spoke and said, "I know a whole lot more than you do, and I don't get on your case". From that moment on, I knew in my heart myself or no one else had perfect doctrines, only the Lord did, yet he never severed a relationship with anyone just because of their doctrine. Yet, despite doctrinal flaws, the Lord still loved us and continued a relationship with us. After all, it was sin, not incorrect doctrine, that affected the relationship with God. From that point in my life, I could accept others in Christ and have a relationship with them, even if their doctrine was not what I believed.

I had committed my life to Christ because of the message of faith. John 14:12 was the scripture that changed my life. I chose a church based on them believing John 14:12, and them preaching faith. I was raised a Baptist, and knew the denominational churches were lacking the faith and the miracles Jesus spoke of. My total adult Christian life was built around faith and the teaching of the charismatic movement during the late 70's, 80's and early 90's.

I began to seriously seek God. Maybe I am wrong. One can interpret the Bible to get anything out of it. I am completely human, so it is possible I have been deceived. I knew lots of scriptures to prove everything I believed, but so did my denominational friends. Almost everyone had scriptures to prove what they believed. I knew you could prove almost anything if you were a talented preacher, or teacher, from the Bible. Teaching the Bible in context was easier to prove false doctrine, than requiring a multitude of scriptures. I knew the Bible could be manipulated. Maybe the devil had deceived me about what I believed.

Because of the doctrinal conflicts with my wife, I really began to seek God. I thought maybe the reason the Lord wanted Veronica and I married was because he knew

Veronica's doctrine was right and mine was wrong. After all, God is merciful to us, if we have a wrong doctrine, I wanted the Lord to make it clear, put it in black and white, and show me what was correct.

I then had a dream. In this dream, I was given a letter. This was a letter from the Lord. Here is basically what it said, it was in black and white:

"... I AGREE WITH THE BOOKS OF DAVID YONGI CHO AND MOST OF THE CHARISMATIC TEACHING. I AM INVOLVED IN BUSINESS AND WANT YOU TO JOIN ME AND WORK WITH ME IN IT. I AM CHARISMATIC. I ALSO DO HEALING MEETINGS. I WANT YOU TO JOIN ME IN DOING HEALING MEETINGS.........."

I was also told in the dream that there had been some confusion and that this letter from the Lord to me and was in response to the letter that I had sent out. I was also shown many people would ridicule it and make fun of it. Yet, I knew it was an answer to the major conflicts that were going on in my life. I knew the Lord sent it, in black and white, to get me out of the confusion and into his perfect will for my life.

The doctrinal issues were clearly addressed. I now knew that Dr. Cho was highly respected doctrinally by the Lord. I now knew, for sure, that the Lord agreed with not only Dr. Cho's books, but most, not all, of the charismatic teaching. I had my answer.

It may not help anyone else, but it answered the question once and for all for me. I would go back and reread Dr. Cho's books. I knew the Lord agreed with them. This time I would read them from a very different perspective.

I also saw very clearly that the Lord was into doing healing meetings. Jesus wanted me to join him in doing healing meetings. This was something that Jesus was doing. It wasn't my idea, it was something from the Lord. The Lord wanted me to do healing meetings. It had been years since I had done healing meetings. I had to repent. To get in the perfect will of God, I must do healing meetings.

CHAPTER XXIV

RETURN TO THE U.S.

I received a phone call from the USA, my favorite aunt Elva had died, and I needed to return to the United States for her funeral. We had been trying to decide if God wanted us to return to the USA or to stay in Chile. It seemed I had no choice but to come back to the USA. God had opened no doors for me in the ministry or to make money.

Since I needed to come back for the funeral, my wife and I decided I would move back to the USA and start preparing for her to return to live in the United States. For this to happen, it meant I needed to be working at some place to make a decent income to show the Immigration and Naturalization Service that I could support a wife.

As a missionary, my income was almost nothing, no one would believe we had been living by faith, on almost nothing. So, I had to go to work for either a secular company or ministry. Since no ministry opportunities came up, I went looking for a job. I found one selling manufactured homes.

About the same time, I had a dream. I heard in the dream "It is a time to accumulate things". To be honest I thought it is about time. I had given and given, it was about time to start receiving.

A few months earlier the Lord had spoken to me in another dream saying, "You have bitterness about not having things". I had to repent about not having stuff. Everyone I knew including the missionaries, all had lots of stuff. But I had given everything I owned several times.

Before God could bring the things to me, I first had to get out of my bitterness about not having things.

Now I would finally start seeing all the things coming to me. I had no vehicle, no house, nothing when I returned.

My Dad had an old pickup he wasn't using much, so he let me use it. At least now I could get to and from work.

I was living with my mother, but I had spent tens of thousands of dollars and a lot of free labor on her house years earlier and took it from an empty, unlivable house to be a comfortable house to live in.

I started my sales job knowing I had to make money and I needed to learn how to sell. They gave me a book and said, "This will tell you all you need to know. Just do it like the book says, and you will be successful." Well it had some very good things in the manual.

But for the first two months I barely made more than minimum wage. But minimum wage was far more than I had been making as a missionary. Yet I was working about 50 – 60 hours a week. I was being diligent but only had a few sales and not much money.

One day my mother mentioned Jerry Bernard was coming to minister at Pathway of Life Church in Dallas.

So, I decided I would go to the meeting. I was tired because of all the hours I had been working. But I felt a leading of the Lord to go to the meeting. I went and at the end of the message, Jerry Bernard began to lead the congregation in singing and worship.

As I was worshipping, the Lord spoke to me, "I am anointing you to sell". Right after this Jerry began to say, "God is anointing someone to sell." I knew this was God confirming what he had spoken to me. I thought this is good. It will be interesting to see what will happen.

Well nothing spectacular happened that I could feel or sense. But the next month I was number one in sales and number one in profit for the company. I made about $8000 in one month. Two months later I was number one again. The Lord was beginning to show me something about the anointing.

I remembered a dream I had in Africa." the station was struggling because it was not anointed". When I saw the difference, the anointing made in something secular like sales I was shocked.

Since I was finally making some money I bought a 2-bedroom house from my grandmother for $21,000 the full appraised value of the house and started working on it. I had to totally renovate it and tear off the back bedroom and add a bedroom and a bath, so it would be a two-bedroom two-bath house of about 1300 square feet. At least it was a start.

Since I was now making good money, I applied for the permanent residence for my wife and we got it. Now she could come here and work.

Our expectations were high. She had been an Operations Manager of a company in Chile and was over about 75 people.

Veronica could not find anything but an entry-level position at any place in the US. She made more money in Chile than in the US.

She was depressed about her life here in the US of A the so called "land of opportunity". The discrimination she faced, the rejection was hard on her. It had her crying on a weekly basis. She took a job making less than what she got paid in Chile.

Since Veronica was frustrated professionally, we began to look for something that would bring satisfaction to my wife, I asked her if you could go back and study and become anything you wanted to do or be what would it be?

She said she wanted to be a nurse or Doctor, when she was young, but couldn't afford to go to school to be a Doctor, and nurses didn't make much money in Chile. So, she decided to study business management and human resources. I had this in my mind, praying over this, wanting something for my wife.

CHAPTER XXV

DAY SPRING WELLNESS CENTER

A friend of mine, Wayne Wilson, called and said Kyle will you go and pray for a friend of mine, Cynthia, to be healed. She only has 2-3 weeks to live. I said yes, I will go and pray for her.

So, I went and prayed for her. She prayed to received Christ and she felt the Lord touch her. I also gave her a couple of my books that I had just printed in Chile including the one on healing.

As the days turned into weeks and the weeks into months, we decided she needed to be baptized in water. We arranged for her to be baptized at a friend's church in Terrell even though she lived in Addison, Texas.

After the baptismal service, we went out to eat with her and her niece. Cynthia began to talk about an alternative health business called "oxygen spas" or "oxygen saunas" that she thought would make a great business.

I began to study this business and discovered that Dr. Otto Warburg, a two-time Nobel Prize winner in medicine, won the Nobel Prize for discovering the cause of cancer and the prevention of cancer. He went on to say that "cancer and other degenerative diseases cannot survive in an oxygen rich environment... the cause of cancer is hypoxia –the lack of oxygen at the cellular level."

This was amazing news for us. We had always been believers in natural ways of healing such as herbs, vitamins and minerals as well as prayer. But this was awesome news. The more I read and studied the more excited we were.

Dr. Warburg and many others proved, that in most circumstances, the body could heal itself, if you detoxified the cells and gave it all the nutritional elements the body needed to rebuild itself. Of course, the number one element the body needed was oxygen.

The oxygen saunas detoxified the body as well as delivered oxygen to the cellular level. Wow! We were impressed with all the information that there was from credible sources. I felt like this might be an answer for Veronica. So, we decided to take the next step.

Veronica and I decided to look for a place and see how much it would cost to set up a place that offered oxygen saunas. I had done my due diligence. I knew the cost of most of the other things, other than the office space. We decided where we wanted to do the office. It was on the I-30 corridor from Garland to Rockwall, this was the area we wanted to be at. So, we went looking to get prices.

We didn't have much money, we were just taking a step of faith in getting all the information together. We needed to know how much we even needed. We knew that was the first step, whether we did it or not. Before you start something, you always need to get all the required information. So, our first step was to get prices and the costs involved. We believed if God wanted us to do this he would provide everything we needed.

The first office building in Rockwall we went to was very expensive, so we decided to drive around looking at buildings on the I-30 corridor in Garland. The second building we went to, had a For Lease sign out front. So, we called and set up an appointment to see the offices with the owner of the building.

As we were leaving the first office suite, the owner of the building asked us what we wanted it for, what type of business and we told him. Then he said, "Well there is a man down the hall that I believe has the same kind of business as you plan to do. But it is strange he paid for a year in advance on his credit card, but I haven't seen him in several months. Do you want to see inside and see if it is the same type of business?' We of course said, yes.

Well we entered his office suite; lo and behold it was the same type of business as we planned. It was equipped, ready and waiting for someone to run it. We were amazed, an entire fully equipped business was waiting for us to find it and to use it.

So, we took a blank invoice off the desk and I contacted him about renting his business fully equipped, with an option to buy in a year. A couple of months later we bought it from him.

Another odd thing in the office suite, in one room there was a nice Plexiglas lectern with pages of healing scriptures compiled on it. I really thought this was a sign that this was to be a place combining prayer with the natural alternatives to bring forth healing spirit, soul and body. Apparently, this was a different type of healing ministry we were getting in to.

We made a deal. We then purchased some other equipment. Veronica and I both became certified OHT's through a program and a Doctor in Canada. We started getting crash courses in everything related to natural health. Within a short time, we were open, doing business and helping people be restored to health. No one could believe the miracle that God had done for us.

The man we bought the business from told us he had been healed of liver cancer using this method and is why he started the business. He thought it would be easy to make good money from it, but the manager he hired to run it, stole money from him and he had to close it.

We could have used it just like it was, but we wanted to upgrade some of the equipment and had to be trained. But God was so good. We started going to meetings that were teaching about different alternative health modalities. We soon discovered and implemented many things such as Hair Tissue Analysis also known as Hair Mineral Analysis that showed people what their bodies were lacking nutritionally, concerning vitamins, minerals and the foods they should eat or avoid. We started doing hormone tests and micronutrient test. We then began to learn the imperatives of colon, liver and kidney cleanses for good health. After this we began to learn about the importance of the proper PH balance.

It didn't matter much how many vitamins and minerals you took if your PH levels were out of balance or your colon was not able to absorb the supplements. The body would only absorb small amounts of them, if the PH wasn't correct or the colon wasn't clean. Also, the PH in the body was like a swimming pool. If you let a swimming pool get too alkaline, all sorts of stuff will start growing in it. If it is too acidic, it becomes corrosive and deteriorates everything quickly that is in it. The PH of the body works in a similar fashion.

At the same time of opening Day Spring, Veronica had to go in for her yearly mammogram. They did the mammogram and the report came back positive. She had a lump about one half an inch behind the nipple. She was concerned, but we both thought, now we get to prove whether all this information and stuff really works. Now there was a personal stake in it.

With the new information, we had about helping the body heal itself, we had to put it into operation. So, we started the Canadian Doctor's protocol for breast cancer.

Veronica was scheduled 4 weeks later for a compressed mammogram. We decided this was enough time for God to do something. We prayed and started the protocol with only the activated oxygen sauna as per the protocol. Every day as Veronica was doing the protocol we could see something was happening to her breast.

The skin started peeling. It changed colors. It began to itch. But all of this was only on the breast that had the lump. The other breast was fine with no discoloration or anything. We took that as a sign it was working. The skin and discoloration looked awful. But we followed the protocol because we knew that many times people have a "healing crisis", with things like that happening, as the body heals itself.

Four weeks later she had the mammogram and the lump was gone, and there was only a slight calcification on the skin. Praise God. We knew first hand, this was of God, and Day Spring would be able to help many people.

The testimonies of how God used this business could fill a book. Our business can't make any healing or cure claims for legal reasons in the USA, only Medical Doctors can legally claim cures or healing. But we have received testimonies from people that had cancers, diabetes, Alzheimer, dementia, bad joints, backs, fibromyalgia, immune system diseases, sclerosis of the liver, eyes, hearing, strokes, weight loss, almost every type of disease.

God was blessing the people with health in a higher percentage, than should have been happening naturally, because of his grace and prayer.

An amazing thing was everything we really wanted or needed in the business God was providing. God was adding so many things to the business. We weren't getting rich but God was providing for us.

One of the many testimonies I will tell about Dayspring and Veronica, came about I believe, because we were going to Christ for the Nations Church. We had heard the testimonies of 8 people that had been raised from the dead. These were from different missionaries, to a Pastor in Georgia, that were speaking at CFNI. Pastor Bozart had invited them to speak at the church.

After hearing these testimonies from people Veronica had a client die in the office. This client had not been experiencing anything she thought was severe, or Veronica would have made her go to the Doctor or an Emergency room. She was walking across our spa room when she collapsed. She stopped breathing. Her eyes rolled back in her head. Her body released urine and feces from it. It was a messy smelly situation.

Veronica quickly went to get the lady's husband, which was across the hall.

Veronica prayed and knew what she should do. She started using the name of Jesus to call the lady back from the dead. She said repeatedly, in Jesus name, Come Back! You cannot die today. Come back in Jesus name... I command you in Jesus name come back.

Life returned to this lifeless body. Immediately she said to Veronica, why did you bring me back. I was in a beautiful place. I was in Heaven. Veronica told her you have a husband and children, you are needed here.

We laughed about the fact that she was brought back to life, and she got mad at Veronica for doing it. Surely only in this country, do people get mad at you, after a miracle is done in their behalf.

Heaven and where she was at was so beautiful, she really

did not want to leave. But the name of Jesus, was more powerful than her desire to stay in Heaven or her desire to continue enjoying the peace and beauty of Heaven.

After seeing someone come back from the dead, some of the other miracles seem small by comparison. Another time this happened as well, when I was there, but the man did not see Heaven.

CHAPTER XXVI

A VISITATION FROM GOD

The Spirit of God has been falling on us in services for about 10 weeks. Grown men began to cry, with no message being preached, just because hands were laid on them, or even at times just sitting in their seats and God's presence overcomes them. The tangible glory of God had fallen over us, as we were giving our pride to the Lord, asking the fire of God to fall and consume the offering of our pride.

People have been repenting, getting healed, words of knowledge have flowed as a river. People have been silent, shouted, cried, jumped and danced. People have been falling to the floor under the power of God, so much so, that our altar area had to be expanded. They would be sitting in their chair and overcome with Gods presence, so much so that they would fall out of their chairs.

People have been letting go of bondages, sin and problems. There has been prophecy accompanied by waves of glory. There had been visions. We have had more people than ever before. People are feeling things and experiencing things they had never felt before.

I even woke up one Sunday morning, still in bed, feeling

the tangible power and glory of God all over me. When I got to church, before the service even started, people would start crying because I merely placed my hand on them, saying nothing. God was doing something sovereign and unexpected.

Christ for the Nation Fellowship of Ministers and Churches is partially responsible let me explain. I had been pushing Chris Juhl, the director of CFN FMC to start a local monthly fellowship for local ministers, so they could be ministered to in the Dallas area.

When we started having the local monthly FMC fellowships, I always came looking for several things. I was looking for people that I thought could help my church. We had a small church, so we needed a lot of things. I was also evaluating people, that I thought I might become good friends with. I was also praying for divine connections. Plus, I also was looking for people I could be a blessing to. The revival, move of God or visitation has come to the church, in large part because of looking for these things in every FMC fellowship meeting. Let me explain.

Along the way, we had become members of Christ for the Nations Church and 3 years later I also became a member of Christ for the Nations Fellowship of Churches and Ministers.

I then left Christ for the Nations Church, when I accepted the pastorate of a small country church in a place I had lived as a teenager.

There were several things as to why this visitation happened. Morne Slabberts, a true man of God, a minister from South Africa and I had met at the ministerial fellowship. He came to the church and started having meetings every Friday Night. He had a miracle and teaching ministry, so we got along great and we flowed together very well. He is part of why the visitation happened.

People in the church did not know it, but I had discovered

the church was stealing money from me, that had been dedicated to me, on their giving envelopes. The church leadership was part of it. But instead of making a big deal out of it, I forgave it and ignored it.

When I took the pastorate, a system was set up where I would get a housing allowance, plus whatever the congregation dedicated to me on their giving envelopes. In this way, my hopes were, no one could complain how much I received from the church. After all the ones that wanted me to get it, gave it.

Well an elder in the church thought I was getting too much money, so he directed only the money given by my personal friends or family to go towards my salary. This went on for several years, before I accidently discovered it.

I have never been in the ministry for money, after all money is just a tool to be used. But this was a new low.

Well as I prayed for these that were involved with the money stolen from me, God began to work sovereignly through me and Morne to bring the manifestation of the Holy Spirit, and for the people to repent. Because I freely forgave is why the outpouring I believe began to happen.

One of the church elders once was sitting in his seat, the Holy Spirit and the glory of God all over him. Tears were running down his checks. Yet you could see he was so angry, he did not want any part of it. He was experiencing the presence of God against his will.

Morne had placed a hand on his shoulder. He was experiencing the power of God, like he had never experienced before, yet he wanted it to stop.

It was very sad. He did not want to change, and his pride stood in the way of letting God work in his life.

What people cannot control or duplicate, they will attack. Since some people could not control what God was doing, or duplicate it, it made them want to attack it and stop it. This happens quite frequently in religious circles.

After Pastoring this church for 7 years we left. This church was quite dysfunctional. There was the stealing from me. I was cussed out in the lobby of the church by church members several times. People screaming at my wife.

The elders never wanted me to invite the previous pastors to come back to the church. I eventually figured out why. They still talked about how bad the previous pastors were even decades later. The sad thing is that the stories of bad pastors were laughable. These people were still mad, decades afterward, because people in the church gave the previous Pastors, personally some money. They said anything given should go to the church. They did not care if the Pastors before had money, to pay their bills. They just wanted the church to have cash in the bank.

The elders that were part of the problem eventually left the church. When they had finally left the church, I was too tired, to build a new church from the ground up, which is what was needed. The only way this church could succeed was with a new core group of people. People that agreed with their Pastor, people that feared God and wanted to please God and that did not have to do things their own way.

This was the strangest place I had ever ministered at. Yes, I knew it was a supposed witchcraft stronghold, with many covens in the area. Yes, I knew it was in the methamphetamine capitol of Texas. Yes, I knew there was a special Texas Ranger task force there, because of the crime and corruption there, but it never explained the response.

People could be getting healed in a service and not come back, or only come back when they needed something. Sometimes there would be standing ovations during a message and the next Sunday 40% fewer people. Any service that experienced the power and the glory of God in manifestation, the following Sunday about 40% fewer people. The people of this church and area, apparently did not like to experience the supernatural and the miraculous that God had for them.

There was a couple of interesting things that happened, that should have woken up a few people. There had been someone with a gun, that shot up the church and some signs the church had in front. Within a few weeks of the event we found who did it. The boyfriend of someone in the church.

We only found out because he died in a four-wheeler accident. People just don't seem to understand, don't mess with the things of God and people of God.

A funny and curious thing would happen in the church auditorium as well. We had a couple of portable air conditioning units, with wheels on them in the auditorium, that we would use occasionally, if it was very hot. The units were plugged into a regular wall plug. These would always work when you turned on the unit from the device itself. The strange thing is they would turn on by themselves, and still show it was off.

Many times, during prayer meetings, they would come on by themselves. You would have to unplug it, to cut it off. Yet plug it back in and it worked perfectly. Check it out and nothing was wrong with it.

The opinion of some was that because there had been so much strife in the church, it opened a door to the devil, or a spirit and the spirit would make it come on, to scare people into leaving the church. I personally think it may have been caused by a reverse polarity in the building, somehow. But maybe they were right, and it really was a spirit. God and the devil both have unexplainable miracles that can be attributed to them.

When Veronica and I left this church, we found out about a Bible study, that Joseph Prince's Ministry was starting in the

US. This would later become Grace Revolution Church.

So, we became very involved with helping to get it started in the Dallas area. The Grace Reigns Bible study was in Los Colinas for about six months. But a church was started in Frisco and then moved to Carrollton and eventually moved to Irving, Texas. After the church had grown to over 1000 people, my wife and I backed off our involvement in the church and became just regular members there. It was fun to me to help start a church even though I was not pastoring it. I love to start things for God.

CHAPTER XXVII

SOLUTIONS FOR THE WORLD TODAY

People are looking for an experience with God, but they don't even know it. They are wanting to experience something new, wanting something different. They are trying new things, always wanting something new, or fresh, so they can have a new experience. They are hungry for an experience that is new and different. They are going from one thing to the next, from one game to the next, from one book to the next, from one church to the next, from one fad to the next. They are thirsting for knowledge, desiring to learn something new, constantly acquiring and achieving, but the experience never leaves them satisfied for long.

Different partners, different careers, different jobs, different addresses, different lovers, different friends have they gave gone after. But they are only satisfied for a short time. Then it is on to the next feeling of newness, that only lasts a little while and then they are empty again. They need to fill the emptiness with something -anything. The emptiness of silence, the emptiness of something is missing, that emptiness that can't be described. That emptiness that is longing to be satisfied.

Some fill the emptiness with drugs, some with money,

some with knowledge, some with subservience, some with affairs, some with thrills, some with College degrees. Some fill the emptiness with anger, while others let the anger turn inward and fill the emptiness with depression. Some fill the emptiness with war and killing, while other fill the emptiness with sexual experiences or even pornography.

Some of the people fill the emptiness with their work, so they become workaholics, some with video games. Meanwhile the addiction rates grow higher. The rates of happiness go lower, dysfunctional families increase, suicides rise, mass shootings increase. Why?

At the core of humanity, deep inside of them, deeper than their soul, there is a place called the spirit of man, longing to be filled with the Spirit of God. It can only be filled with the One, that created man. When man was created, God created an emptiness in him, that only God can fill. It is only when we are filled with God, can we truly be satisfied and content in this life. Anytime in this life that we feel empty, it is because God is wanting us to open ourselves more to him. God will fill us with himself and his Spirit, if we open our mind, our soul, our heart and spirit.

God sees your emptiness, yes, God created it in Adam and Eve. He did not create this emptiness to make man miserable, or for man to become workaholics and drug addicts, murders and thrill seekers. He created it, so man would turn to him. God created man to communicate with himself and together, man -the individual and God, could do great things together. This emptiness was created, so we would seek God, be filled with God and together with God, we would do great things. The Bible declares, in the New Testament and the Old Testament, that we should say, The Lord is my helper, the Lord is on my side, I will not fear, and that he will never leave us.

When that emptiness or the frustration, or that sense of not being content comes, you need to ask yourself four questions.

Question 1. Is God in you? Have you asked God's son Jesus to enter your inner most being, your heart or your spirit?

If you haven't, say in your own words, Lord Jesus come into my heart and cause me to be born again. Jesus come and fill the emptiness inside of me. Come and live in me. Come into my flesh, into me, and I ask you to forgive me of all my sins. My sin has kept you from living in me, forgive me of all my sins, and come and live in me. I want an experience of you living in me, of you helping me, of you being on my side. I want to experience the joy of fresh for-giveness. I want to experience the cleanness and that sense of righteousness that you offer. I receive it now.

Just give yourself to the Lord and then receive him into your life. Start a 2-way relationship with God. Give yourself to him and let him give himself to you.

Anytime you don't feel that God is in you, focus on being forgiven. Awareness of sin or awareness of missing it, or awareness of doing wrong, makes us feel as if we are alone. If we feel we are alone, and feel that God is not with us, we open the door of our heart to misery.

This is the reason he said, I will never leave you... so that you can say the Lord is my helper. The more we focus on God loving us, that God is with us and that he has forgiven us, the more it makes us aware of his presence, within us. Christ in us is the hope of glory. Start seeking the experience of God in you.

Question 2. Have you been filled with the Holy Spirit since you believed? This is a question Paul, in the Bible (Acts 19), asked people that were believers. When you are full of the Spirit, you are full of God and therefore full of love, joy, peace etc.

Have you experienced being filled with the Holy Spirit and are you still full? If you are not full of love, joy and peace you need to be filled or refilled with the Holy Spirit.

The Bible (Ephesians 5) says we are filled, in the continuous sense, by singing and making melody in our hearts to the Lord. If you are not full, ask the Lord Jesus Christ to fill you with the Holy Spirit. Then begin praising and worshipping God. Seek this worship experience of getting filled with the Holy Spirit. As you start worshipping God, giving to God, he will start giving back to you, -His Spirit, His love, His joy, His peace, His gifts of the Holy Spirit.

Question 3. Is there a relationship God is wanting
you to get into?

At first the main thing is a relationship with God.
This is what God wants us to focus on, but as we
grow an emptiness will reappear, when God is wanting us to get married, become part of a church or is
trying to put someone new in our life.

Adam was empty and sensed something was
missing,without Eve, even though he had God.
Something was still missing. Sometimes the
emptiness is a sign that God has a family or some
type of relationship, that is needed in our lives.
Without a church family or a physical family -people
will often feel empty.

Listen to the emptiness to guide you into complete-
ness that creates contentment. There may be a
greater God ordained relationship waiting for you to
experience. It might be a spouse, but maybe a best
friend.

Are you content with your church, your friends, your
marital state. A spouse was never intended to fill
the space of God or being filled with the Spirit or
of being filled with your purpose or job assignment
from God. Don't expect a spouse or relationships to

fill your emptiness alone. We are more complex than that.

Question 4. Is there a God assignment waiting for you?

Jesus the son of God, who is God, said my meat to eat is to do the will of God. There will be an inner emptiness if you never have an assignment from God to do. When you are not content, ask the Lord and yourself, is there a God assignment I should be doing? Doing an assignment or preparing to do an assignment in God's eyes is the same. Is there something I should be preparing myself to do, or something He wants me to do?

Many times, when we experience emptiness, it is because God has a new assignment for us to do. When we are bored with life, depressed, dissatisfied with life or angry, or you want to go back to drugs, alcohol, or sex -ask yourself something.

When was the last time you heard from God, or had a God assignment? When was the last time you truly felt content, inside of yourself? When is the last time you were filled with joy, with joy coming from inside of you? When was the last time you had an experience with God?

Emptiness comes when God is ready for us to grow, and we are ready to take the next step in life. That emptiness is a reminder God has something more for us. Let that emptiness be your guide to greater experiences with God. When you learn to recognize emptiness as the sign for something new ahead, something waiting for you from God, some new experience with God, you will live an exciting and fulfilled life.

The Islamic World

Even though our focus is not anti-terrorism, it is a reality in the world today. Let's look at the roots of Islamic terrorism. Many US sociologists say that Islamic terrorism is from the extreme poverty. If you don't do something about their, (the radicals) poverty, nothing else matters. I think it is important to do things to relieve pain, poverty and suffering everywhere we go, for Jesus did. But my experience says it is not the answer to the problem of Islamic terrorism and Islamic expansion.

What I was told about the history of Islam, from those in West Africa who practice Islam, They said something like this. Mohammed reportedly became disillusioned with Christianity because of all the sin, hypocrisy and corruption he saw in Christianity. So ultimately Islam was birthed, because of hypocritical Christians. True believers in Islam are supposed to respect Christians, those that are true believers and that live the life.

Islam grew and grows today, mainly because the Christians

compromised their lifestyle and their message, at least according to those in Islam, I spoke with. They often point to Hollywood as the example of Western society excesses of sin. They point to the lifestyles, dress and attitudes of western society Christians.

Yet when they see miracles happening before their eyes they turn to the Lord in droves. I have been in places such as the town of Kenema, Sierra Leone, where Evangelist Eric Cowley had healing crusades that were so powerful, no one was in the mosques for a week or so. There were all at the healing crusades. To impact Islam, the gospel with the miraculous must be presented. An intellectual gospel will not reach Muslims causing them to convert. They must see the power of God.

Some have become disillusioned with Islam and the hatred and violence associated with Islam. Inside their heart, they know that it is not the way. But the only way to reach them is with the power of God. Guns and violence won't change them. You must show them changed lives, holiness, prosperity and the miracles if you want lots of Moslems to convert to Christianity. They will respond to true spiritual power, not military power. Any spiritual people, such as the Moslems, Taoist or even Buddhists, must see spiritual power, to make them want to follow someone else other than Mohammed or Buddha. Spiritual power is what we need to show the followers of Islam and Buddha. The power to heal the sick and cast out devils. The power in Jesus name.

The Ayatollah of Iran called the President of the USA the head of the Great Satan. The reason for this is Muslims do not see US Presidents pray and fast. They don't see him publicly call for repentance. They don't see him renounce greed and covetousness or sexual immorality. These are things they believe someone spiritual will do.

The Muslims are hungry for spiritual leaders, that

demonstrate their spirituality. Whereas most Christians, hide their Christianity. But when the body of Christ, rises up in power and holiness, then in every country where it happens, you see mass numbers come to Christ from Islam and other religions. The best defense against Islamic terrorism is to preach the full gospel with holiness, signs, wonders and miracles combined with Christian leaders being vocal against sin and injustice.

A US president calling for a time of repentance, fasting and prayer will do more to make Islamists rethink that America is the great Satan, than all the bombs in the world.

The Spiritual World

Most people are unaware of the spiritual world that rules and controls, the physical and even political world. One of the most powerful things for a person to do, is to pray in the spirit or pray in tongues. I know of stories where people started praying for their President and individuals, at the exact time something was happening, not knowing their life was at stake, and miraculously their life is spared.

What I am about to say is so dramatic, that many psychiatrists would say a lot, about this statement, I am going to make. I know what they would say, and I would normally agree with them, if I had not lived and experienced it myself. Sometimes your experiences with God can defy worldly logic.

Here is the statement. One individual praying in tongues, with the help of the Holy Spirit can change countries, nations, governments and heads of states. I have seen two governments change through military takeovers and two democratic elections for heads of state, be changed, helped or caused, through praying in tongues or intercession in tongues.

When this has happened with me, there were several

factors involved. This has happened with myself on 3 different continents. I will not go into specifics of which governments, or politicians this happened with, for merely revealing it, would make it become political. It is something spiritual. The most important thing is, you must have the country in your heart and not just want something in your head.

I was shocked when I discovered who God had me interceding for, to become President of a country in South America. It was not someone I would have chosen, to even vote for. As I was praying in tongues, I began to see, after weeks of interceding in tongues, as to why he should be President. God did it to help the poor of that country.

In another country, a military Captain started a rebellion accidently, simply because he wanted his guys and himself to be paid. They had not been paid in six months. He became the head of state at 28 years of age, because he stood up for his men, and stood up against a corrupt General. He did not plan on becoming head of state. It was God's plan. God did want it, I saw how praying in tongues worked an amazing story with the Captain that became a head of state in one week's time. The intercession took months.

When you pray in tongues you can only be praying the will of God, and you are praying for so many things that are involved, in causing something to happen, that the people involved have no clue, they are being influenced spiritually to do and make some of the decisions they make. This is why praying in tongues for some things, takes months of intercession, before something takes place.

In another country, a person God wanted to be elected was a terrible politician, but apparently, a good businessman. He would make so many mistakes. After about 3 months I realized my praying in tongues was for him. He was far from perfect, but for some reason God wanted him in office. This man's poll numbers would go down and God would have me interceding in tongues for days. They would go back up. Every time I stopped praying in tongues, his numbers would go down. Every time I would be praying in tongues, his numbers would go up. It was amazing to see this at least 8 times over many months. I have always liked politics, but never have I seen such a bad politician, yet God wanted him in office as head of state.

This type of intercession is not something you choose. Apparently when you pray in tongues a lot, God will give you an assignment that your praying in tongues, is to accomplish. Apparently, sometimes to accomplish a goal, it is linked to a person or persons praying in tongues.

U.S. President Barak Obama once said, you have the elected officials you deserve. Here is a thought. What if God left good governance in the hands of His people and said, I have given you authority and gifts, now use them. I will allow the Holy Spirit to pray my will into existence, creating the governments and elected officials God really wants.

I first used the principle of praying in tongues to build a house for my mother and myself. Years later I accidently discovered that praying in tongues could create new governments and even influence elections. So, I believe, based on my experience, the solutions for so many of the problems in the world has a solution, to be found and experienced by praying in tongues.

One last note, I have learned by experience the Holy Spirit needs something in your heart, before he starts interceding about it. You cannot dictate to the Holy Spirit, what or who you will intercede for from your intellectual mind. It must be a desire, he sees in your heart, that is in line with God's will.

There are a lot of times I would say to my wife, why doesn't God help me in this situation or that, and I saw no help, even though I was praying in tongues.

Even a friend of mine said Kyle, I will not pray in tongues over my business deals any more. Every time I do they fall apart.

Why? Because something is not in the will of God. Only when your desire lines up with God's will, can the prayer in tongues line up for your benefit. If things go bad when you pray in tongues, ask the Lord to help you get in his perfect will.

The Intellectual World

As the old saying goes there are no atheist in fox holes. The meaning here is that when the people were under military fire, facing death, they would turn to God. Many would say most intellectuals are atheists, but I disagree.

When a person claims, they are an atheist, and they get angry about people believing in God, they are almost always a believer in heart, that is simply mad at God. It is hard to be angry at something you, in your heart, don't believe in.

Everyone knows the world is round, but if a few people say it is flat, would you get angry? Of course not. People get angry about something, because they have a vested interest in it. Would you get angry if I said 2 plus 2 equals 5. No, you would merely think I was ignorant.

An angry atheist is usually a true believer, that covers up their belief, with their anger. They are truly angry at God. Therefore, they are a believer in God. You cannot be angry at someone, you do not believe exists.

True intellectuals take a scientific approach and simply do not believe in God, because scientifically, he has not been proven to them. The term for this is agnostic, not atheist. An atheist does not believe in God, but an agnostic is one that when shown real evidence will believe in God.

A true atheist will never believe, even if shown and knows God's existence is proven. So, true intellectuals are neutral about the existence or lack of existence of God.

So, a true intellectual is agnostic, not an atheist. An intellectual will let their intellect, and their experiences, and the evidence prove if there is a God. A real atheist will never believe even if shown the truth, and it is proven. So, a real intellectual must be agnostic, or a believer in God.

So, what is the answer to bring intellectuals to Christ. It is simple. Messages about Christ is not what proves things to them, after all, they have their ideas and reasoning as well as you. A superior argument rarely wins them over. The best way to win an intellectual is through power evangelism.

Power evangelism is using the power of Jesus Christ, bringing God's power to the intellectual or the person you are talking to, and showing them that Jesus is alive, and Jesus is still doing miracles today. Show them power and miracles that defy logic, let them experience God, and you will see them convert to Christ. I have seen so many people get saved and pray to receive Christ because they got healed or saw others getting healed. There are few agnostics left in a meeting after they have seen many miracles, done in the name of Jesus Christ, before their own eyes.

Jesus showed himself alive by many infallible proofs, to the people in Israel, about 2000 years ago. That generation needed to see the miracles to believe in him. That was not the intellectual age in which we live in and are entering into now. The people were simpler then, but the answer is the same. People, especially intellectuals that are agnostic, need to see infallible proofs that Jesus is alive and a miracle worker. Every generation needs to see the miracles and evidences and experiences, that Jesus is alive.

I really don't blame intellectuals, and so many people, for not believing in God. The ministers and priests had a responsibility to offer gifts to God, and then in turn minister the gifts from God to people. Gifts from God to people such as miracles, healings, prophecy, etc. reveal God to man. God gave these gifts to the church, so the church could show them to the world. Now in this age ministers merely give gifts to God and rarely minister gifts from God back to the people.

Churches were to be a place of the miraculous, a place of healing, but many have become Christian social clubs and learning centers. They have not been the place where ministers minister the gifts from God to the people. They have become a one-way street with praise, prayers and worship to God, but rarely is it a 2-way street where God himself gives gifts to people.

Your relationship with God must become a 2-way relationship, you to God and God to you, or you will get tired of the farce of Christianity, tired of the rituals of Christianity, tired of the exercises of Christianity, tired of the legalism or the politics of Christianity.

God designed the religion of Christianity to resemble the power and miracles of Jesus Christ, as he walked on earth. As the Bible declares Christ, the power and the wisdom of God, even so Christianity should declare the power and wisdom of Jesus Christ himself, to a dying, suffering, agnostic world.

If you have never had an experience with God, ask the Lord now to show himself alive to you by infallible proofs. You have a right to have a proof of his existence. Ask Jesus now for some miracle, such as a healing or a divine intervention, that will be able to help someone you love, or help you in some way.

Ask the Lord to put in your mind a simple prayer, that he can answer, to prove to you he is alive. Let the Lord give you a sign of his power and that he is alive. Ask him to put in your mind the sign, or the prayer he wants to answer, that proves he is alive. After you have that simple prayer in your mind, from the Lord, ask him to do it and then write it down. Read it every day until it happens. When it happens, you need to tell some people what God did for you. Jesus is waiting to show himself alive to you.

CHAPTER XXVIII

I HAVE A DREAM

A preacher named Martin Luther King preached a message that went around the world. It was "I Have a Dream".

I too have a dream. I have seen the sick and suffering people in Africa, South America, North America, and in the Caribbean. I have seen the need of teaching in Europe, Africa, South America, Central America, the Caribbean, and the United States. I have seen the thousands of people pray to receive Christ, and are as lost sheep, because they don't receive the follow up they need. I have seen people at judgment day crying out "If I had only known, if I had only known, if I had only known". I had seen the rich suffering and being empty inside, because they didn't have a good relationship with the Lord. I had seen the poor crying out, because of their poverty. I had seen the sick, crying out in pain.

If I had any compassion, if I had any mercy toward others, if I had a heart that could be touched with the feelings of people's infirmities, if I truly had the love of God in my heart, if I truly had been born again, I must work to fulfill my dream. I must go and teach all nations. I must reach out to suffering humanity. I must take Christ to the nations. I must take his power to the nations. I must show and demonstrate the power of God to a lost, hurting dying world. I must ignore my pain. I must ignore my sacrifices. I must ignore my desires. I must reach out to the hurting masses of people. I must do all that is in my power. I must do more than is possible. I must build a foundation of support that will endure, for I have a dream.

I have a dream, I believe it is God's dream of teaching all nations through books, radio, TV, the internet and in person. I have a dream of seeing a Christian Bible institute in every nation of the world. I have a dream of seeing Christian radio stations in every city in the world. I have a dream of teaching people of every language and every tribe. I have a dream of taking God's healing power to the people of the world. I have a dream of helping the hurting. I have a dream of teaching the ignorant. I have a dream of healing the sick. I have a dream of reaching the lost. I have a dream of seeing people be born again. I have a dream of people becoming mature Christians. I have a dream of people living holy lives. I have a dream of seeing people prospering by the power of God. I have a dream of seeing people get excited about the things of the Lord. I have a dream and I believe it is of the Lord.

Do you have a dream of reaching the lost? Do you have a dream of healing the hurting? Do you have a dream of reaching the suffering? Do you have a dream of delivering people from hell? Do you have a dream of touching the lives of people in every nation of the world? Do you have a dream of letting God lead you to help change the world? Do you have a dream? Do you have God's dream? I believe this is God's dream.

How can we change the world? How can we deliver people from hell? How can we get people saved? How can we get people healed? How can we relieve the suffering? How can we help them that are sitting in darkness and the shadows of death? How can we take God's power to a lost, suffering,

213

dying world? How can we do it?

We must have a plan. God always has a plan. God has a plan to save the world. God has a plan to relieve the suffering. God has a plan to save people from hell. God has a plan to heal the hurting. God had a plan he gave to Noah. God had a plan he gave to Moses. God had a plan he gave to Abraham. God had a plan he gave to Joshua. God had a plan he gave to Gideon. God always has a plan of salvation. God always has a plan to relieve the suffering. God always has a plan.

I have a plan. I believe it is God's plan. For this plan saves the lost. This plan heals the hurting. This plan delivers from death and hell. This plan reaches the poor and suffering. This plan reaches the rich and wealthy. This plan brings the plan of salvation. This plan produces Christians. This plan produces growth and maturity. This plan, I believe, is from the Lord.

Jesus had a plan. Jesus told his plan to the disciples. He said go and preach the gospel throughout all the world. The plan of Jesus was a plan of reaching the world. We must have a plan of reaching the world. Does your plan include reaching the world for Christ? Does your plan go into the uttermost parts of the earth? Is this your plan? Is this your dream? It is my dream. It is Jesus' dream. Will you join us in this dream?

My dream needs poor people and rich people. My dream needs baby Christians and mature Christians. My dream needs intercessors and preachers. My dream needs administrators and teachers. My dream needs engineers and janitors. My dream needs little ministries and large ministries. My dream needs the famous and the unknown. My dream needs lawyers and accountants. My dream needs politicians and presidents. My dream needs doctors and farmers. My dream needs mechanics and construction workers. My dream needs YOU.

I can't fulfill my dream without you, but I believe my

dream is of the Lord. I believe this is Jesus' dream. Will you join us in our dream?

Our dream starts wherever we are. Our dream starts with what we have. Our dream has already begun, but our dream needs you. Will you help us expand our dream? Will you join us and be partners in our dream? Without you, our dream will fail. Without you, the dream of Jesus will fail, for Jesus had a dream. He had a dream of going into the entire world. He had a dream of reaching every person.

Will you let my dream become your dream? How will you go into the entire world? Take hold of my dream. Let us go into the world together. Hand in hand, heart joined to heart, let us go forth into all the world.

Do you have the dream? Has it taken root yet? Has Jesus planted his dream in your heart? Let us go into all the world together, you and I. The vision is waiting. Souls are dying. The suffering continues. The cries for help continue. The world is suffering. Will you help? What is your part? Do you have the vision yet? Do you have the vision of a lost, suffering dying world? Is Jesus speaking to your heart? Are you ready to reach out to a lost, suffering, dying world? Can you hear the cries of the suffering? Can you hear the cries of the dying? Can you hear the cries of the lost? Can you hear them say, "If I had only known, if I had only known, if I had only known"?

I have seen it. I know it is true. Can you hear their cries? Can you see their suffering? Have you caught the vision? Do you want to help reach out to a lost dying world? The vision is waiting for you.

Jesus is waiting for you. Join me in reaching out to the people of the world. We can do it together. Hand in hand. Shoulder to shoulder. Marching. ONWARD CHRISTIAN SOLDIERS. Let us go to war. The battle is waiting. The victory is ours. The heathen are waiting. They are the spoils of war.

www.ingramcontent.com/pod-product-compliance
Lightning Source LLC
Chambersburg PA
CBHW071526040426
42452CB00008B/902